A
CLASSICAL
PRIMER

Dan Crompton studied Classics and Linguistics at Cambridge University and lives in London. He wishes someone had given him this book when he was a student.

He has also published *A Funny Thing Happened on the Way to the Forum* (2010), a translation of the oldest joke book in the world.

A
CLASSICAL
PRIMER

ANCIENT KNOWLEDGE
FOR MODERN MINDS

DAN CROMPTON

MICHAEL O'MARA BOOKS LIMITED

First published in Great Britain in 2012 by
Michael O'Mara Books Limited
9 Lion Yard
Tremadoc Road
London SW4 7NQ

A CIP catalogue record for this book is available
from the British Library.

Papers used by Michael O'Mara Books Limited are natural,
recyclable products made from wood grown in sustainable forests.
The manufacturing processes conform to the environmental
regulations of the country of origin.

ISBN: 978-1-84317-880-4 in hardback print format
ISBN: 978-1-84317-898-9 in EPub format
ISBN: 978-1-84317-897-2 in Mobipocket format

1 3 5 7 9 10 8 6 4 2

Designed and typeset by www.glensaville.com

Printed and bound in Great Britain by Clays Ltd, St Ives plc

www.mombooks.com

CONTENTS

CONTENTS

INTRODUCTION

For a few people, the mere mention of Classics will trigger monochrome memories of facing the blackboard with books on their heads for posture, chanting out meaningless conjugations of *amo*, *amas*, *amat* in unison. For the vast majority, however, there will be no such associations, and Classics will merely be that subject that was studied at posh schools that look like Hogwarts.

To save you looking it up, let us say briefly that Classics is the study of the culture of the Ancient Greeks and Romans, and takes in all aspects of their life and learning – from the languages to their literature, philosophy, art, history, sciences, politics, religion and all sorts. Through their texts, buildings and monuments, both civilizations have left us (literally) heaps of information about how they lived. But the real fascination in the subject doesn't come just from being immersed in their lives, but also by realizing just how many aspects of our own daily life have been directly influenced by theirs.

Everyone knows that the Romans built roads. But we can also thank both empires for bringing us central heating, concrete, the twelve-month calendar, plumbing, heated swimming pools, cranes and – most crucially – pizza. That's not to mention the cultural benefits such as laws, a welfare system, philosophy and language. And, without ancient mythology and literature, Shakespeare would barely have strung a sentence together.

The Greek empire at one point stretched as far east as India, and the Romans once had control over most of Europe, the Near East and northern Africa. The Greeks made sense of the stars, figured out π, gave us $a^2+b^2=c^2$, and even managed to work out the circumference of the Earth. It took the rest of the planet centuries to emulate any of these achievements (Columbus did not confirm that the Greeks had been quite right about the Earth's being round till 1,700 years later), and there is no doubt that our world without these Greek and Roman influences would be a very different place.

Back in the good old days of the last century (I hasten to add this is several decades before I was born), having a sound Classical education was deemed a jolly good thing. In the face of its rapid demise, this book is intended to give anyone who has an interest in knowing about the basis of our own culture an insight into the key influences we can thank the Greeks and Romans for.

Any reciting of *amo, amas, amat* will be entirely voluntary.

DAN CROMPTON

CHAPTER 1

GREEK AND LATIN
LANGUAGES

The Greek language: from Alpha to Omega

Ancient Greek is not an easy language to master. However, its influence over so much of our language today means that it deserves a few moments to pick up the basics – at the very least so that you might be able to recognize the difference between a ταβερνα and an ακροπολις on your next holiday.

HISTORY

The oldest surviving form of Ancient Greek is Mycenaean Greek, which used an alphabet now known as Linear B from as early as 1600 BC. Scholars spent years trying to decipher Linear B from remnants unearthed in Crete, Mycenae and elsewhere, and it wasn't until 1952 that its syllabic letters were finally cracked.

The current Greek alphabet, derived from Phoenician, didn't appear for another 800 years or so, in about 800 to 700 BC. (The Phoenicians were an ancient civilization based around the eastern Mediterranean and beyond, who had important trading and cultural influences across the whole region from around this time. Whole books could be written on them – and indeed have been – but we really must crack on.) The mountainous mainland and the isolation of the country's islands meant that many dialects of the language were able to exist side by side for many centuries, until a common Greek (Koine Greek) was settled on in the fourth century BC. This was probably as a result of Alexander the Great's incredible expansion of the Greek empire during this time (all the way to India), which required tens of thousands of soldiers to come together and be coherently governed with one common language.

THE ALPHABET

You'll be pleased to hear that it won't take decades of research to pick up the basics of the alphabet, though, and we'll have you reading simple words in no time. In these examples, you'll see how many of the words we use today are derived from Ancient Greek words – or, in some cases, straightforward transliterations of the original word.

There will be no vocabulary test at the end.

Greek letter	Alphabet symbol	Closest equivalent in English	Used in a Greek word
Alpha	A, α	*a* in *pathetic*	παθητικος (pathetikos) capable of feeling
Beta	B, β	*b* in *barbarian*	βαρβαρος (barbaros) foreign
Gamma	Γ, γ	*g* in *grammar*	γραμμα (gramma) letter
Delta	Δ, δ	*d* in *domestic*	δομος (domos) house
Epsilon	E, ε	*e* in *exit*	εξοδος (exodos) way out
Zeta	Z, ζ	*z* in *zoo*	ζωον (zo-on) animal
Eta	H, η	long 'eh' sound as in *air*	αηρ (aer) air
Theta	Θ, θ	*th* in *theology*	θεος (theos) god
Iota	I, ι	*i* in *plinth*	πλινθος (plinthos) brick
Kappa	K, κ	*c* in *catastrophe*	καταστροφη (catastrophe) an overturning
Lambda	Λ, λ	*l* in *lamp*	λαμπας (lampas) torch
Mu	M, μ	*m* in *mathematics*	μαθησις (mathesis) education
Nu	N, ν	*n* in *Nike*	νικη (nike) victory
Xi	Ξ, ξ	*x* in *toxic*	τοξον (*toxon*) (poisoned) arrow

Omicron	O, o	*o* in *topical*	τοπος (topos) place
Pi	Π, π	*p* in *epic*	επος (epos) word
Rho	P, ρ	*r* in *rhythm*	ῥυθμος (rhythmos) rhythm
Sigma	Σ, σ, ς	*s* in *symbol*	συμβολον (sumbolon) sign
Tau	T, τ	*t* in *technology*	τεχνη (techne) skill
Upsilon	Υ, υ	*u* in *prune*	προυμνον (proumnon) plum
Phi	Φ, φ	*ph* in *philosophy*	φιλοσοφια (philosophia) love of wisdom
Chi	X, χ	*ch* in *loch*	χριστος (christos) the anointed one, Christ
Psi	Ψ, ψ	*ps* in *Cyclops*	Κυκλοψ (kuklops) round eye
Omega	Ω, ω	long 'oh' sound as in *ochre*	ωχρος (ochros) pale

NOT AN IOTA OF DIFFERENCE

On top of these twenty-four characters, there is a whole heap of accents called *diacritics*. They began to be seen in texts from about 400 BC onwards in answer to some of the ambiguities in the language. They can appear on any of the seven vowels in the alphabet and are used to denote either tone of the vowel or stress on the syllable.

Luckily for modern Greeks, the tonal diacritics were officially scrapped in 1982 (probably for being far too confusing). Unfortunately for students of Ancient Greek, we need to know the difference between the letter η with no diacritic, and one with an iota subscript (ῃ). And the less we say about the differences between ἤ and ῇ, the better. In fact, the letter η on its own can have about six different meanings, dependent on the placement or not of the various diacritics.

The only diacritic that perhaps you should pay attention to is the aspiration, which is almost like a very small *c*-shape that can be placed over any of the vowels and also over a Rho as in ῥ (rh), ἁ (ha) or ἑ (he). The aspiration gives any letter a breathing *h* sound, which doesn't exist as a letter in Greek in its own right. This gives us the silent *h* in many English words that are derived from Greek, such as *rhythm*. For simplicity, I have left out all diacritics from this book except for the aspiration.

A QUICK TRIP TO HONOLULU

Way back in the twentieth century, an American linguist discovered something truly staggering in the Greek language: when comparing some of the language's basic words, he found remarkable similarities with similar words in the Hawaiian language.

Observing the list of words below indicated some ancient link between the two languages.

HAWAIIAN		ANCIENT GREEK	
aeko	'eagle'	αετος (aetos)	'eagle'
no'ono'o	'thought'	νοος (no-os)	'mind'
mana'o	'think'	μανθανω (manthano)	'learn'
mele	'sing'	μελος (melos)	'melody'
lahui	'people'	λαος (laos)	'people'
meli	'honey'	μελι (meli)	'honey'
kau	'summer'	καυμα (kauma)	'heat'
mahina	'month'	μην (men)	'month'
kia	'pillar'	κιων (kion)	'pillar'
hiki	'come'	ἱκανω (hikano)	'arrive'

I know what you're thinking: what on earth is going on? Is it possible that the Ancient Greeks took a wrong turn on the way to Athens and accidentally found themselves on Waikiki Beach?

Alexander the Great managed to extend the Greek Empire all the way to India, but even he would have had quite some difficulty making the 8,000-mile trip to Hawaii, teaching the locals some Greek words, and heading back in time for dinner. Keeping the holiday a secret from any historians would also have been tricky.

A few theories have been put forward to explain this linguistic phenomenon. And the one that most academics have settled on is quite possibly the most irritating: it is just a coincidence. I won't go into any more detail than that, since we're clearly wasting our time.

THE GRAMMAR BASICS (IN ANY LANGUAGE)

You may have heard some rather scary things about Latin and Greek grammar. But I can assure you that there are some simple basics that will help you understand how the languages work with only minimal effort. Long tables of verbs and nouns can be daunting – but, when put into context, they need not be anything to fear. First, a quick look at how the Latin and Greek (and indeed English) languages are structured.

Different languages structure sentences in different ways. In English, we rely very heavily on the order of our words to dictate what is going on. So, in the very different sentences 'Jack loves Jill' and 'Jill loves Jack', you can tell who is loving whom by the order of the words. Latin and Greek tend not to care a jot for word order, so have to use other indicators to let you understand what on earth is going on.

Verbs in the languages use different endings to indicate who is doing that verb, and the nouns also have different endings depending on what function in the sentence the noun represents. This means that the words can be placed in almost any order, and you can clearly see which nouns and which verbs fit together from their endings. So in the Latin equivalent of 'Jack likes Jill', the words could be in any order, but you can tell who is doing what by the different endings on the words.

In Latin, *puella* means 'girl' and *puer* means 'boy'.

So: *puella amat puerum* means 'the girl loves the boy'
But: *puellam amat puer* means 'the boy loves the girl'

The number of different inflections of verbs and nouns means that the teaching of Classical languages tends to involve lots of tables. The unfortunate truth is that one of the most effective ways of learning the rules is simply by repetitious reading (yes, out loud) of the verb and noun tables, which is perhaps why Latin gets such a bad rap in school.

NOUNS: THE CASES

Nouns serve different functions in different sentences. If you consider the sentence:

Jack gives the ball to Jill in the garden

it is clear that Jack, Jill, the ball and the garden all have a different role to play in the meaning of the sentence. In English, word order and prepositions ('to Jill', 'in the garden') let us know what function each word has. Latin has divided its nouns into six different functions (or cases), and Greek has divided its nouns into five basic functions, each of which can have different endings to show which case they are.

1. NOMINATIVE

This is the **subject** of a sentence – the word that is doing the main action. In the sentence above, 'Jack' is the nominative. We get the word 'nominative' from the Latin *nomenare* ('to nominate'), as this word has been given the title of head of the sentence.

2. VOCATIVE

This arises when we are **speaking to** someone – 'Oi, Jack!'
The word 'vocative' is from the Latin *vox*, meaning 'voice' (the
English word 'voice' comes from the same root).

3. ACCUSATIVE

This is the **object** of a sentence – the word to which the main
action is being done. In the sentence above, 'the ball' is the
accusative, as it is the object of the main verb. In English, we
can see the accusative case in words such as 'him' and 'her' (as
opposed to 'he' and 'she').

The word 'accusative' clearly comes from the same root as
the English 'accuse', and originally indicates motion against
something.

4. GENITIVE

This usually describes **possession** – if you can say 'of' before the
noun, it's probably genitive. So, in the phrase 'Jack's ball' (or 'the
ball of Jack'), Latin and Greek would pop 'Jack' in the genitive.

The word 'genitive' is from the same root as 'generate',
'general' and even (excuse me) 'genitals', and indicates origin.

5. DATIVE

This is an **indirect object** of a sentence – if you can say 'to' or 'for' before the noun, it's probably dative. In the sentence above, 'to Jill' puts her in the dative.

The word 'dative' is to do with giving things to someone – and is from the same root as English words 'donate' and 'date' (see p. 46 for more details).

6. ABLATIVE

Bit of a funny one. It often indicates **motion away from**, as well as being used with a lot of common prepositions like Latin *ex* ('out of'), *in* ('in') and *cum* ('with'). If you graduate *magna cum laude* in the USA, you are doing so 'with great praise'. The words *magna laude* are both in the ablative following *cum*.

The ablative does not exist in Greek. Instead, its functions are mainly swallowed by the Greek genitive. The word 'ablative' comes from the Latin *ablatus*, which literally means 'carried away'.

So in the example sentence above:

Jack	gives	ball	to Jill	in the garden.
nominative	verb	accusative	dative	ablative

LATIN NOUN DECLENSIONS

Latin nouns generally fit into one of five different declensions – that's five slightly different ways that the cases can appear. They can also be masculine, feminine or neuter in grammatical behaviour. The logic for some verbs having a gender is clear (as in *puella* for 'girl' and *puer* for 'boy'), but in most nouns it just indicates which grammatical patterns that word will follow. In very basic terms, many feminine nouns end in *–a*, many masculine nouns end in *–us*, and many neuter nouns end in *–um*.

It is conventional to read these tables (out loud) down the page, with singular first and then plural.

1ST DECLENSION (FEMININE)

puella 'girl'

	Singular	Plural
Nominative	puell–a	puell–ae
Vocative	puell–a	puell–ae
Accusative	puell–am	puell–as
Genitive	puell–ae	puell–arum
Dative	puell–ae	puell–is
Ablative	puell–a	puell–is

So, in the sentences below, you can see how the accusative ending on *puell–am* in the second example makes her the object of love, rather than the subject of the sentence:

1. *puella amat puerum* means 'the girl loves the boy'
2. *puellam amat puer* means 'the boy loves the girl'

2ND DECLENSION (MASCULINE OR NEUTER)

servus 'slave' (masculine)   *bellum* 'war' (neuter)

	Singular	Plural	Singular	Plural
Nominative	serv–us	serv–i	bell–um	bell–a
Vocative	serv–e	serv–i	bell–um	bell–a
Accusative	serv–um	serv–os	bell–um	bell–a
Genitive	serv–i	serv–orum	bell–i	bell–orum
Dative	serv–o	serv–is	bell–o	bell–is
Ablative	serv–o	serv–is	bell–o	bell–is

Masculine nouns in the 2nd declension end in *–us*, and give us the delightful plurals used in English like 'cacti' and 'octopi'. Some people refer to the plural of female restaurant staff as 'waitri', but I can assure you this is incorrect.

Neuter nouns in the 2nd declension end in *–um* in the singular and *–a* in the plural, with the same ending in nominative, vocative and accusative. Here you can see why in English we use plurals ending in '*–a*' for 'bacterium', 'forum', 'medium', 'equilibrium' and many other words taken from Latin.

GENDER STEREOTYPES IN LATIN GRAMMAR

It's a strange circumstance that feminine 1st-declension nouns have no separate ending for the vocative case, whereas the 2nd-declension masculine nouns do have a distinction. It is also worth noting that neuter nouns of any declension have the same ending for nominative, vocative and accusative (both singular and plural). Exactly the same principles can be seen in Greek masculine, feminine and neuter nouns (see pp. 39–42), as well as in several other languages.

A theory to explain this is that male-dominated ancient societies aimed their education, philosophy, politics and literature towards men. They had much more use for a vocative case to differentiate between speaking *to* a man and speaking *about* him. The need for differentiation could have been less so among women, who were kept away from public philosophizing and discussions.

Similarly, the inanimate objects that fall under the neuter gender tend not to be the active participants of a sentence – they instead have things done *to* them. For this reason, it becomes less important to differentiate between the nominative and accusative, as context will do the explaining for you. Neuter nouns, therefore, can get away with having the same endings in these cases without causing any confusion about who is the subject of the main verb.

The theory isn't watertight by any means, but is one way of looking at why noun endings in Latin, and indeed many other languages, are the way they are.

3RD DECLENSION
(MASCULINE, FEMININE OR NEUTER)

miles 'soldier' (masculine)   *opus* 'work' (neuter)

(feminine endings are the same)

	Singular	Plural	Singular	Plural
Nominative	miles	milit–es	opus	oper–a
Vocative	miles	milit–es	opus	oper–a
Accusative	milit–em	milit–es	opus	oper–a
Genitive	milit–is	milit–um	oper–is	oper–um
Dative	milit–i	milit–ibus	oper–i	oper–ibus
Ablative	milit–e	milit–ibus	oper–e	oper–ibus

Third-declension nouns are a bit different, as they have a slightly different word stem from the accusative or genitive onwards. As before, however, the neuter nouns have the same endings in the first three cases. The plural of *opus* is where we get the name for musical operas in English.

Interestingly, the *–ibus* ending seen here in the dative plural is still used in English and other languages the world over. The Latin plural dative of the word *omnis* ('all') is *omnibus*, meaning 'for everyone', and it is from this word form that we get the word 'bus'.

There are also 4th- and 5th-declension nouns in Latin (tables below), but I will stop there as I can see someone at the back nodding off.

4TH DECLENSION
(MASCULINE, FEMININE OR NEUTER)

manus 'hand' (feminine)　　　　*cornu* 'horn' (neuter)
(masculine endings are the same)

	Singular	Plural	Singular	Plural
Nominative	man–us	man–us	corn–u	corn–ua
Vocative	man–us	man–us	corn–u	corn–ua
Accusative	man–um	man–us	corn–u	corn–ua
Genitive	man–us	man–uum	corn–us	corn–uum
Dative	man–ui	man–ibus	corn–u	corn–ibus
Ablative	man–o	man–ibus	corn–u	corn–ibus

5TH DECLENSION (ALMOST ALL FEMININE)

res 'thing'

	Singular	Plural
Nominative	r–es	r–es
Vocative	r–es	r–es
Accusative	r–em	r–es
Genitive	r–ei	r–erum
Dative	r–ei	r–ebus
Ablative	r–e	r–ebus

VERBS

Well, here it is. I did promise in the introduction to this book that there would be no reciting of *amo, amas, amat.*

I lied.

(I could of course have chosen another verb as a demonstration of Latin conjugation, but it seems wrong to veer away from an old favourite that will have any linguaphobe quietly turning over to the next chapter.)

Similarly to nouns, Latin verbs also have endings to help you understand who is doing what in the sentence. Below is the irregular verb *esse* 'to be' (which is always very handy) as well as the old favourite regular verb *amare* 'to love', just to give the flavour of how Latin verbs work.

	esse 'to be' (irregular)		*amare* 'to love' (regular)	
I	sum		am–o	
you (singular)	es		am–as	
he/she/it	est		am–at	
we	sumus		am–amus	
you (plural)	estis		am–atis	
they	sunt		am–ant	

The first person singular ('I') always ends in –*o*, as in the English word 'video' (meaning 'I see') or the old-fashioned dog's name 'Fido' (meaning 'I trust').

The third person singular ('he/she/it') ends in –*t*, as in the English word 'exit' ('he goes out') or 'caveat' ('may he be careful'). (*Caveat* is actually in the subjunctive mood, which is used to indicate possibility or hypothetical action.)

Going back to the earlier examples, you can see how *puella amat puerum* means 'the girl loves the boy', but, if more than one person were doing the loving, you'd need a plural word ending: *puellae amant puerum* means 'the girls love the boy'.

Latin verbs are a whole feast in themselves, and the tables of verb endings continue relentlessly to indicate different tenses, moods and voices, but I think we'll leave them here for now and press on with the basics of the Greek language.

EVERYONE'S SPEAKING THE SAME LANGUAGE

You may notice from the forms of the Latin regular verb *amo* that there are some similarities in endings with modern European languages, such as French, German and Spanish.

The *–s* ending for 2nd person singular ('you') is common in many languages; the *–mus* ending for 1st person plural ('we') can be seen in the Spanish *–mos*; and the *–nt* ending for 3rd person plural ('they') is also seen in French. There are even some clear similarities with the regular Greek endings (as on p. 43).

As demonstrated in the first chapter, languages often borrow from one another, giving us English vocabulary rooted in words from Latin, Greek, Norse or any number of other origins. However, it's not just vocabulary that we borrow: the very structure of language can be shared across very wide areas. You can see similarities in verb, noun and adjectival endings (as well as vocabulary) not only across Europe but across most Indo-European languages – all the way over to the ancient Indian language Sanskrit.

THE GREEK GRAMMAR BASICS

THE 'THE'

The first thing to learn in Greek is the definite article (otherwise known as 'the'). The forms of the definite article have similarities with noun and adjective endings throughout Greek, so are a good basis for getting to grips with the rest of the language. If you get the definite article down, then you're laughing. (Or crying, depending on how long it takes you.)

As before with the Latin tables, it is conventional to learn this case by case from left to right (ὁ, ἡ, το). There is no vocative case in the definite article.

THE DEFINITE ARTICLE ('THE')

Singular	Masculine		Feminine		Neuter	
Nominative	ὁ	ho	ἡ	heh	το	to
Accusative	τον	ton	την	ten	το	to
Genitive	του	tou	της	tes	του	tou
Dative	τῷ	toy	τῇ	tay	τῷ	toy

Plural	Masculine		Feminine		Neuter	
Nominative	οἱ	hoy	αἱ	hay	τα	ta
Accusative	τους	tous	τας	tas	τα	ta
Genitive	των	ton	των	ton	των	ton
Dative	τοις	tois	ταις	tais	τοις	tois

The accents (diacritics) shown here change the sounds of the vowels a little bit. The *c*-shaped diacritic above ὁ and ἡ puts an aspiration before the vowels, making them sound like 'ho' and 'heh'. The subscript iotas in the singular datives (τῳ, τῃ, τῳ) sound as though they have the iota letter (ι) placed after them, giving you 'toy', 'tay', 'toy' sounds.

You may be familiar with the English phrase 'hoi polloi' – often used by complete berks to refer to the general population. The original is from the Greek οἱ πολλοι (pronounced 'hoy polloy'), meaning 'the many'. The word οἱ is the definite article for words in the masculine plural, as you can see in the table. And πολλοι means 'many' and is the same word we get the English prefix 'poly-' from, for words like 'polygon', 'polymorphic' and 'polyester'.

Now that you know how the Greek definite article works, you can correct anyone who refers to 'the hoi polloi' for using too many definite articles.

NOUNS

The good news about Greek nouns is that there are just three declensions. In very basic terms, many feminine nouns end in –η ('–e'), many masculine nouns end in –ος ('–os') and many neuter nouns end in –ον ('–on'). These are cognate with the Latin –a, –us, –um endings.

The bad news is that most of the nouns used in Greek don't really fit into these declensions properly and that it can sometimes seem as though every word were an exception to the rule. But the brave reader should give this a go, and you'll be reading simple sentences in no time at all. (And no worries if you want to go back to the start of Chapter 1 for guidance on the Greek alphabet.)

1ST DECLENSION

(MOSTLY FEMININE, BUT SOME MASCULINE)

τιμη ('tim-eh') (feminine): 'honour'

Singular			
Nominative	ἡ	τιμ–η	he tim–eh
Vocative		τιμ–η	tim–eh
Accusative	την	τιμ–ην	ten tim–en
Genitive	της	τιμ–ης	tes tim–es
Dative	τη	τιμ–η	tay tim–ay

Plural			
Nominative	αἱ	τιμ–αι	hay tim–ay
Vocative		τιμ–αι	tim–ay
Accusative	τας	τιμ–ας	tas tim–as
Genitive	των	τιμ–ων	ton tim–on
Dative	ταις	τιμ–αις	tais tim–ais

This feminine noun uses the feminine definite article from the previous table, and shows how similar the endings can be. This is why learning the definite article upfront gives you a firm base from which to learn the rest of the language.

Incidentally, the word τιμη ('timeh') is where we get the boy's name Timothy from. It is combined with Greek θεος ('theos'), meaning 'god', to describe someone who honours their god.

2ND DECLENSION
(MOSTLY MASCULINE AND NEUTER,
WITH A FEW FEMININE EXCEPTIONS)

λογος ('logos') (masculine): 'word'

Singular			
Nominative	ὁ	λογ–ος	ho log–os
Vocative		λογ–ε	log–e
Accusative	τον	λογ–ον	ton log–on
Genitive	του	λογ–ου	tou log–ou
Dative	τῳ	λογ–ῳ	toy log–oy

Plural			
Nominative	οἱ	λογ–οι	hoy log–oy
Vocative		λογ–οι	log–oy
Accusative	τους	λογ–ους	tous log–ous
Genitive	των	λογ–ων	ton log–on
Dative	τοις	λογ–οις	tois log–ois

Because λογος ('logos') is masculine, it is paired with the masculine definite article here. Once again, you can see how the endings match. As with Latin masculine nouns in the 2nd declension, there is a distinctive ending for the vocative case.

3RD DECLENSION
(MASCULINE, FEMININE, NEUTER)

πραγμα ('pragma') (neuter): 'deed, act'

Singular			
Nominative	το	πραγμα	to pragma
Vocative		πραγμα	pragma
Accusative	το	πραγμα	to pragma
Genitive	του	πραγματ-ος	tou pragmat-os
Dative	τῳ	πραγματ-ι	toy pragmat-i

Plural			
Nominative	τα	πραγματ-α	ta pragmat-a
Vocative		πραγματ-α	pragmat-a
Accusative	τα	πραγματ-α	ta pragmat-a
Genitive	των	πραγματ-ων	ton pragmat-on
Dative	τοις	πραγμασ-ι	tois pragmas-i

This is a neuter example of a 3rd-declension noun, and, as in Latin and many other languages, the neuter always has the same form for nominative, vocative and accusative in both the singular and plural.

VERBS

Greek's equivalent of *amo, amas, amat* is in the verb λυω ('luo'), which is always the first verb that students learn. It's a bit of a strange piece of vocabulary with limited use, but its structure is wonderfully regular and allows you to see how the basic verbs behave.

εıμι ('eimi') 'I am'   λυω ('luo') 'I loosen'
(irregular)   (regular)

I	ειμι	eimi	λυ–ω	lu-o
you (singular)	ει	ei	λυ–εις	lu-eis
he/she/it	εστι	esti	λυ–ει	lu-ei
we	εσμεν	esmen	λυ–ομεν	lu-omen
you (plural)	εστε	este	λυ–ετε	lu-ete
they	εισι	eisi	λυ–ουσι	lu-ousi

Similarities with Latin can be seen in the –ω ending for 1st person singular ('I') and –ς ending for 2nd person singular ('you'), and there are a few other indicators in these endings that can be seen in many Indo-European languages should you wish to delve deeper.

Without wanting to put a dampener on things, let me say that Greek verbs are a pain. Learning the basics will take you a fair way, but it's not long before all the exceptions to the rule begin to creep out of the woodwork, so we should quit while we're ahead.

GREEK AND LATIN:
QUOD ERAT DEMONSTRANDUM

There is a wealth of phrases from Latin that are still used in their original form as part of the English language. Some are very familiar to us (such as *carpe diem*), while others we use all the time perhaps without realizing their Latin origins (for example '*e. g.*'). This chapter explains some of the more common phrases that are still in use.

Latin phrase	Literally means	And in English
a priori	'from the previous'	An idea you held in your head prior to what experience might tell you. You may have had an *a priori* assumption that Latin was no longer in use.
ab initio	'from the beginning'	From the beginning.
ad absurdam	'to the absurd'	Taking a logical argument to its extreme conclusion in order to disprove it. In Chapter 5, you'll see how the Greek philosopher Zeno did this *ad absurdam*.
ad hoc	'to this (thing)'	Something that is for a specific purpose – an *ad hoc* committee can be an impromptu one set up for a particular reason.
ad infinitum	'to infinity'	Continuing to carry out an action *ad infinitum* would probably bore you after a while.
ad nauseam	'to sickness'	Likewise, repeating something *ad nauseam* is likely to leave you feeling less than chirpy.

addendum	'(a thing) that is to be added'	Something added onto a note or document.
		We get the English word 'add' from the same root, and the ending '–endum' shows this is a gerundive. I won't bore you with the details, but it puts a sense of obligation onto the verb. Incidentally, in case you want to be fancy, the plural of this is *addenda*.
affidavit	'he has pledged'	A written statement used for evidence in court.
		The word is a combination of *ad* + *fido* ('to be faithful' – which is where the old-fashioned dog's name comes from).
agenda	'(things) that are to be done'	A running order for a meeting.
		Just like *addendum*, this is a gerundive. The root verb *ago* generally means 'to do' and is where we get words like 'agitate' and 'act'.
		It is a plural noun, so you can be fancy by referring to a single item on the running order as an 'agendum'. Don't blame me if no one knows what you're talking about.
alma mater	'nourishing mother'	Your school, university or other formative institution.
		Originally this referred to any number of female deities, but someone in a straw boater must have once coined it for a university. A number of universities in the US have taken it a bit too literally by erecting statues of an actual nourishing mother figure.
ante bellum	'before the war'	Antebellum wistfulness seems to follow most wars, and is not specific to any particular one.

bona fide	'in good faith'	Genuine.
		This is the same *fido* ('faith' or 'trust') as in *affidavit* above.
carpe diem	'seize the day'	A well known phrase. The word *carpe* is an imperative, telling you to do something. Preferably today.
		(For the origin of the phrase, see the section on Horace in Chapter 4.)
caveat	'may he be careful'	An additional warning or advice.
		It's also a verb in English now, so you can caveat your advice to someone by telling them you might be wrong.
circa	'around'	From the same root as the word 'circle'. Anything that lies near enough to the thing you're talking about.
compos mentis	'in control of the mind'	Having all your capacities and being clear-thinking.
curriculum vitae	'the course of life'	We now either shorten it to CV, or in fact borrow from another language with the French *résumé*.
data	'given (things)'	Information or statistics.
		'Data' is actually a plural noun, so to be pompously correct, you should use a plural verb with it too ('I think you'll find these data *are* incorrect, Professor Lambsbottom').
		The singular is *datum*, which was used on Roman letters with the location to show where it was 'given' to a messenger. This led to the plural *data* referring to both the location and day that a letter was handed over – which is where we derive the English word 'date' from.

GREEK AND LATIN LANGUAGES

deus ex machina	'god from the machine'	This is a device used in theatre, literature or film in which the story is suddenly resolved by an unexpected (and convenient) event. The phoenix at the end of the first *Harry Potter* book springs to mind. It comes from the physical machinery in Greek and Roman theatre that would lower a god onto the stage from the heavens in order to quickly sort everything out before the last bus home.
e.g. (exempli gratia)	'for the sake of example'	For example.
ergo	'therefore'	Therefore. Often used by comic-book enthusiasts trying to prove a point. Its popularity may stem from its use by seventeenth-century French philosopher Descartes, who used the phrase *cogito ergo sum* ('I think, therefore I am').
forum	'a public place'	Any open platform for discussion (physical or digital). It is worth noting once again that the proper plural is 'fora'. We get the word 'forensic' from the same root – meaning evidence that is suitable for a public hearing.
i.e. (id est)	'that is'	Used to further explain a point.
in memoriam	'in the memory'	In memory of something.
in situ	'in the place'	Something in its original place.
in vino veritas	'truth in wine'	The embarrassingly honest witterings of a wine-fuelled night have caught many of us out.

ipso facto	'by the fact itself'	By that very fact, or therefore.
mea culpa	'through my fault'	Used mainly in Catholic prayer. It is in the ablative case, meaning it is *through* my fault' that the sins have been committed. For extra guilt, you can add *mea maxima culpa*.
modus operandi	'way of working'	The way in which you do something. The word *operandi* is once again a gerundive (like *agenda* and *addendum*), as it implies a degree of obligation in the verb.
non sequitur	'it does not follow'	Something that doesn't follow what precedes it. I'm also partial to a spot of cake.
NB (nota bene)	'note well'	A fact that deserves special attention.
per centum	'of a hundred'	Often abbreviated to 'per cent' (or 'percent' in the US), or the % symbol (made up of two zeros and a division line to show division by 100).
per se	'of itself'	Essentially or intrinsically.
quasi	'as though'	Something that resembles a certain quality. Used as a prefix to nouns, adjectives and adverbs.
quid pro quo	'something for something'	Exchanging an object or service for one of equal value. If you want to refer to multiple things being exchanged, you could use '*quae pro quibus*', but that may be verging on the ridiculous.
QED (quod erat demonstrandum)	'which was to be demonstrated'	Said after a point has been demonstrated to be true.

re:	'about the thing'	This is seen in email subject headings the world over. It is the ablative case of *res* ('thing'), so translates as 'about the thing' following the colon.
sic	'in this way'	Newspapers and other publications use this to show that any grammatical or factual errors in quoted text were in the original and have been deliberately left unchanged.
status quo	'the state in which'	The general current state of a situation. Also a popular British rock band.
verbatim	'word by word'	The suffix *–atim* is a nifty tool that changes the meaning of nouns like *verba* ('word') to mean 'word by word'. Also seen in *gradatim* to mean 'step by step'.
vice versa	'with the position being reversed'	The reverse order of a previous statement.
vox pop (vox populi)	'voice of the people'	Used in broadcasting to refer to short interviews with 'the man on the street' for his opinion.

A huge chunk of our language also comes from Greek, with many words we use every day coming direct from the streets of ancient Athens – from *philosophy*, to *catastrophe*, to *drama* and *comedy*. But, with the different alphabet in Greek, it's a bit harder to find exact transliterations of whole expressions that are used directly in English today.

However, there are plenty of expressions that we use in English that are lifted straight from Greek philosophy, literature and mythology that have elbowed their way into our cultural psyche.

Achilles' heel	The hidden weak spot of a person or situation. The original Achilles was dipped into the River Styx in the Underworld as a baby to make him immortal. Unfortunately, his mother Thetis dunked him in by holding his heel, which was the one place that he could be killed. Rookie mistake.
Electra complex	A term coined by psychiatrist Carl Jung to refer to a state of female sexual development, which may result in someone's being what might euphemistically be referred to as a 'daddy's girl'. The corresponding male complex is known as the Oedipus complex (see below). The original Electra plotted with her brother Orestes to kill their mother Clytemnestra for murdering Agamemnon, their father. (More of her tragedy in Chapter 3.)
epic	This is used to describe any lengthy or grand undertaking. The Greek work επος ('epos') means 'word', and originally referred only to epic poetry (such as Homer's *Iliad*) which centres on a hero and his achievements.
eureka	This exclamation is used by mad cartoon scientists the world over at the point of a major discovery. It is the perfect past tense of εὑρίσκω ('heurisko' – 'to find') so means 'I have found (it)'. Archimedes apparently shrieked it out as he ran through the streets of Syracuse naked, having realized in the bath how an object displaces its own volume in water when submerged. By measuring the weight of the king's crown, and then seeing whether it displaced the same amount of water as the same weight of pure gold, he was able to test whether a goldsmith had sneakily replaced any of the gold with a cheaper metal of different weight. Water submersion is still the definitive way to measure the human body fat index, based entirely on Archimedes' discovery.

Herculean effort	Hercules accidentally killed his wife and children (Zeus's wife Hera was in a mood, so made Hercules go a bit bonkers). To atone for his sins, he undertook twelve near-impossible tasks, mainly killing multiheaded mythical creatures. Most images and statues of the hero have him wearing the hide of the Nemean Lion, which he strangled in the first of his twelve labours.
I know one thing – that I know nothing	Plato's writings focus on the philosophical teachings of Socrates (more about them in Chapter 5). This is one of Socrates' most famous statements, and demonstrates his method of challenging what we think we know in order to allow the student to dissect a philosophical question.
Know yourself	The Greek phrase γνωθι σεαυτον ('gnothi seauton') was inscribed over the entrance to the Temple of Apollo at Delphi, in which the famous gibbering Oracle would give her advice and premonitions.
Midas touch	Midas was granted one wish, and he chose that everything he touched would turn to gold. The reality, of course, was a complete kerfuffle – with food, drink and even his daughter all turning into gold. Our modern meaning rather alarmingly refers only to the positive short-term gain and tends not to reference the fact that Midas nearly starved to death and immediately regretted his power.
Odyssey	This is used nowadays to mean any long journey. The first was undertaken by Odysseus on his ten-year journey back home to Ithaca from the War of Troy (more on him in Chapter 3).
Oedipus complex	The male psychological complex coined by Freud, corresponding to the Electra complex (above). The original Oedipus was disowned at a young age by his parents (the King and Queen of Thebes) when it was prophesied that he would kill his father and marry his mother. Not knowing that he is related to them, he ends up fulfilling the prophecy. A bit of a mess. (More on him in Chapter 3.)

The face that launched a thousand ships	When Helen (later Helen of Troy) was abducted by Paris, it heralded the start of the ten-year Trojan War. This phrase is from Marlowe's sixteenth-century play *Doctor Faustus*.
Xmas	Some purists resent the use of 'Xmas' for 'Christmas', believing the *X* to be an algebraic substitution for 'Christ'. However, it in fact comes from the Greek letter χ ('chi') for χριστος ('christos'), which means 'the anointed one'.

ANCIENT WORDS FOR MODERN MEANINGS

Many English words are taken direct from Greek transliterations – some examples of which can be seen in the Greek alphabet section. However, we have also taken sections of Greek words to make our own compound nouns for modern inventions.

The word 'helicopter', for example, is made up of two Greek words: ἑλιξ ('helix') and πτερον ('pteron').

ἑλιξ ('helix') is a spiral, and πτερον (pteron) is a wing, describing the way that a helicopter takes flight. When it's used in a compound noun, it is common to take the genitive root of a noun, which in this case would be ἑλικος ('helikos').

The word πτερον ('pteron') is the same root used in the dinosaur 'pterodactyl' (literally meaning the dinosaur that had fingerlike bones in its wings). Its original meaning was 'feather', and it is in fact the same root as the word 'feather' in English, as well as therefore the word 'pen'.

If there's only one thing you take from this, make it that from henceforth you hyphenate the word 'helico-pter' in such a way as to show its true etymology if you ever need it to fit across two lines of text.

Another interesting use of ancient language for modern appliances is in the TV. The word 'television' is a curious hybrid of languages, from the Greek τηλε- ('tele') meaning 'far off', and the Latin *videre* meaning 'to see'. The mixture of origins is perhaps because the proper all-Greek version had already been used for 'telescope'.

(In a quick aside to the twentieth century, Hitler famously wasn't a fan of most things foreign, and insisted on abolishing as many non-German terms as possible. He therefore insisted on the translation of the term for television into the literal German equivalent – *fern*, meaning 'far off', and *sehen*, meaning 'to see'. The term stuck and *Fernsehen* is still used in German today.)

THE ROOTS OF MODERN WORDS

The chances are that someone at school once told you that learning Latin and Greek will 'give you a good basis for learning all other languages'. While there is more than a dollop of truth in this, it may be easier said than done to master two ancient tongues before you even begin applying them to your study of other European languages.

So, to make it easier for you, this useful list shows just a handful of affixes and definitions from both Latin and Greek that are in very common use in the English language today. You'll recognize these word segments in your everyday language and will quickly see that your Latin teacher may have been right about his classes having some use.

Affix or root	Language	Meaning	and in English...
ad-	Latin	to, at, towards	admire ('wonder at something') advert ('turn towards something') When paired with some words, this prefix assimilates with the word it is joining and loses the 'd' – as in 'accent', 'accelerate' and, indeed, 'assimilate'.

acro-	Greek	top, peak, high	acropolis ('top of the city') acronym ('a name from the top [letter of each word]') acrobat ('high walker')
alg-	Greek	pain	analgesic ('pain killer') nostalgia ('homesickness')
ambi-	Latin	both	ambidextrous ('both hands') ambiguous ('doing both things')
amphi-	Greek	both, on both sides	amphitheatre ('round theatre') amphibian ('living a double life')
andro-	Greek	man	androgynous ('like a man and woman') android ('manlike')
ante-	Latin	before	ante meridiem ('before midday') antenatal ('before birth')
anthropo-	Greek	human, of mankind	anthropology ('the science of mankind')
anti-	Greek and Latin	against	antidote ('remedy' [against poison]) anti-hero ('opposite of a hero')
bi-	Latin	two	biplane ('two wings') binocular ('two eyes')
bio-	Greek	life, course or way of living	biography ('writing of [a] life') biology ('study of life')
caco-	Greek	bad, evil	cacophony ('bad sound') cacodemonic ('of an evil spirit')
cata-	Greek	down, against, inferior	cataclysm ('wash down', hence a deluge or flood)
circum-	Latin	around, round about	circumcise ('cut round') circumnavigate ('sail round')
con-	Latin	together with, in combination	confide ('to have faith in') conjunction ('joining together')

demi-	Latin	half	demi-monde ('half-world') demi-tasse ('half-cup') – both from French; *see* semi- *below*
dynam-	Greek	power	dynamic ('active, energetic, forceful')
dys-	Greek	bad	dysfunctional ('working badly') dysentery ('bad stomach')
endo-	Greek	within	endocardial ('within the heart') endogamous ('marrying within [a group]')
eu-	Greek	good, well	eucalyptus ('well covered') eulogy ('good words')
exo-	Greek	outside	exodus ('a going out') exogamous ('marrying outside [a group]')
-gram	Greek	written	telegram ('written from afar)
-graph	Greek	written, drawn, recorded	tachograph ('recording speed') typographic ('recorded impression')
gyno-	Greek	woman, female	androgynous ('male and female') gynocracy ('rule by women')
hetero-	Greek	other (of two)	heterodox ('other [unorthodox] opinion') heterosexual ('of the other sex')
homo-	Greek	same	homogeneous ('of the same kind') homosexual ('of the same sex')
hyper-	Greek	over, beyond, excess	hyperbole ('thrown beyond') hyperboreal ('of the extreme north')
hypo-	Greek	under, beneath	hypodermic ('beneath the skin')
in-	Greek and Latin	into, in, within	infest ('fix or fasten in [something]') investigate ('search or enquire into')

inter-	Latin	between, among, amid	intercede ('come between, intervene')
			international ('between nations')
intra-	Latin	on the inside, within	intramural ('within the walls' [of a city, building, organization])
			intranet ('internal computer network using Internet technology')
macro-	Greek	large, long	macrobiotic ('long-living')
			macrocosm ('great world')
micro-	Greek	small	microbiology ('study of micro-organisms')
			microclimate ('climate of very small area')
-morph	Greek	having a particular form or character	morph ('genetic variant of an animal')
			polymorphic ('having many forms')
neuro-	Greek	nerve	neurology ('study of the nervous system')
			neurotic ('suffering nervous disorder')
-(o)logy	Greek	written, said, spoken	theology ('study of god[s]')
			trilogy ('three written [works]')
oxy-	Greek	sharp, keen, acute, acid	oxygen ('becoming acid, acidifying')
			oxymoron ('sharp and dull or stupid', hence 'a contradiction')
peri-	Greek	round, around	perimeter ('measured around', 'circumference')
			perinatal ('[period] around birth')
phono-, -phone	Greek	voice, sound	phonograph ('written with sound')
			telephone ('sound from afar')
photo-	Greek	light	photograph ('written [i.e. delineated] with light')

poly-	Greek	many	polysyllabic ('having many syllables') Polynesia ('many islands')
post-	Latin	after, behind, afterwards	postscript ('written afterwards') post-war ('after the war') posthumous ('after death [literally, 'after burial']')
pro-	Greek	before	proactive ('acting before')
re-	Latin	back, again	reorganize ('organize again') return (literally, 'turn back')
sci-	Latin	know	science ('knowledge')
semi-	Latin	half	semicircle ('half a circle') semi-skilled ('only half or partly skilled') – *see* demi- *above*
sub-	Latin	under, below	submarine ('beneath the sea') substandard ('below the standard')
super-	Latin	above, on top of	superstructure ('built above')
tom	Greek	cut	anatomy ('a cutting up') atom (from ἄτομος, *atomos*, 'indivisible') tonsillectomy ('tonsil cutting [out]')
trans-	Latin	across, beyond, through	transatlantic transfer ('bear or carry across')

CHAPTER 2

CLASSICAL

HISTORY

Greek and Roman history in a nutshell

The amount of literature written on classical history probably covers enough paper to *papier-mâché* over the whole of the Greek and Roman empires completely. The ancient civilizations themselves even had historians writing volumes on their past.

So, instead of delving into the depth of each battle and *curriculum vitae* of every ruler (there were a lot of both), I will take you on a roughly chronological journey from the start of Greece as we know it to the fall of the Roman Empire, taking in a few sights along the way.

THE BRONZE AGE:
MINOANS AND MYCENAEANS

Early forms of writing existed in Greece from about 1600 BC in a script called Linear B (see Chapter 1), but it wasn't until the eighth and seventh centuries BC that the Greek alphabet as we know it came into use, and that writing and literature began to work their way into the society. This means that stories and descriptions of Greek culture and history before this time were written many centuries later, and become somewhat tainted by enthusiastic imaginations and myth.

Excavations in Knossos on Crete revealed a huge sprawling palace dating from about 2200 BC, which has been suggested as being the home of King Minos (leader, therefore, of the Minoans, although this word was only coined in the twentieth century). The palace can be seen today with huge frescoes and structures carefully reconstructed. The legend of Theseus entering a labyrinth to battle the half-bull Minotaur with nothing but a gold thread to help him out of the maze probably arose from Minos's extensive palace and reputation for being a bit beastly.

Since the Minoans weren't Greek by origin, the story of overcoming the mythical monsters from abroad was probably also a nice way to give credence to Theseus, who is perceived as being the founder of Athens and, in fact, most things Greek. Given that the unification of the state of Attica under Athens was a long process drawn out over hundreds of years (and all the way up to the fifth century BC), I will make the assumption that Theseus is more a metaphor for this period rather than one actual man.

After the Minoans vanished (several archaeologists suspect due to a massive tsunami) came the era of the Mycenaeans, from about 1600 BC to 1200 BC. The epic poems of Homer and most of the Greek tragedies are based on events during this time (even if they were composed several hundred years later), and they depict the area of Greece as being made up of many city-states led by kings in enormous palaces. The ruins of the palace at Mycenae are an astonishing sight even today, and are the site of many fantastic legends. It is here, for example, that Agamemnon is said to have been killed by his wife Clytemnestra upon his return from the ten-year War of Troy. (More on that in the tragedies of Chapter 3.)

THE DAWN OF DEMOCRACY

From the eighth century a series of aristocratic kings ruled Athens, followed by some particularly fierce tyrants. With the help of nearby Sparta, the Athenian aristocrats were able to seize power again, and did so in a way that gradually gave the populace more control over the governance of Attica.

In 507 BC the political leader Cleisthenes divided the state into ten regions, each made up of one hundred smaller political units called δημοι ('demoi'; singular 'demos'). The population in these δημοι were were given a new sense of freedom and ownership over the state that it had not had before under traditional monarchic rule, allowing any issues of state importance to be put out to the people for debate first. It is from here that we get the word 'democracy', by combining the singular δημος and κρατος ('kratos' – power).

It should be noted, however, that the ancient definition of democracy may not be how we understand it today. The right to vote in Athens was given only to adult men whose parents were both Athenian, so it is estimated that this may have given the democratic rights to just 15 per cent of the population. While that may seem like a fairly poor effort, it represents a pivotal moment in shaping human society, and it is truly astonishing that these sorts of levels weren't achieved in the UK until the mid-nineteenth century.

This new age of polity heralds the start of the classical period of Greece's history, also known as its Golden Age. This is from around 500 BC to 300 BC, when much of its great literature, theatre, architecture, philosophy and science came into existence.

THE MACEDONIAN EMPIRE: ALEXANDER THE GREAT

Centuries of internal and external wars followed Cleisthenes, but, by 337 BC, Philip of Macedon had managed to defeat many of the Greek states into submission, and took control of Athens in Attica relatively peacefully. Philip invited delegates from most of the mainland states to Corinth, where they formed one union as Greeks under the Corinthian League, and promptly declared war on Persia.

Philip was almost immediately assassinated, but his twenty-year-old son, Alexander of Macedon II, stepped straight into his shoes. Within just a few years, Alexander had conquered the Persians in most of what is now Turkey, Israel and northern Egypt (where he founded the first of many cities he called Alexandria – this one is still one of the country's largest conurbations).

ALEXANDER'S CONQUESTS

He continued marching, and, by 325 BC, Alexander the Great (as he was quickly known) had conquered an area covering modern-day Iran, Afghanistan, a bit of Tajikistan (if you can point to it on a map, you win a prize), and Pakistan before deciding to make his way back towards Greece. Considering that even the individual Greek states had difficulties forming an alliance, it's not bad going to make that alliance stretch so far that it touches India within just a matter of years. His spectacular achievement as a military leader was stemmed only by the dwindling of his men's fervour to keep marching further east away from home.

In 323 BC, Alexander caught a fever and died. The news tipped the balance of the fragile Athens, and the Corinthian

Alliance once again descended into fighting. The result of which was a return to a more aristocratic rule with fewer democratic rights for the general population.

Through much of its archaic and classical history, Greece is less of a nation and more a series of alliances between several states – usually for military reasons. The Delian League (based on the island of Delos from 477 BC) and Philip's Corinthian League are just two of these, and enabled the Greek-speaking states to form large armies against a common enemy without necessarily having to totally surrender their own independence.

THE BEGINNINGS OF ROME:
ROMULUS AND REMUS

If I may skip back (and west) a bit, we can see what was going on with the Romans while Greeks were fighting, growing and fighting again.

Most school students will know the story of Romulus and Remus being brought up by a wolf, but perhaps not how (or why) the myth was chosen to depict the origins of Rome. I'm sorry to say that I'm none the wiser, and I dare say the Romans weren't either. It seems that the twin boys were deserted by their father Mars – the god of violent war – and were brought up in the woods by a wolf (again, an icon of fear).

Romulus killed his brother in an argument and founded a city to celebrate, to which he gave his own name in 753 BC. The only thing left to complete these noble beginnings was to populate Rome with women, which he did by stealing them against their will from nearby Sabinum – a scene captured in countless pieces of Renaissance art as the rape of the Sabines.

It certainly feels like strange beginnings for such a proud civilization. But perhaps it is this sense of pride (to the point of arrogance) that made the Romans so successful: their sense of superiority allowed them to take what they wanted and to expand the empire with great strength. Where Alexander the Great failed with his empire, the Romans were able to instil this glorious sense of belonging within their citizens that lasted a great deal longer. The violent myths of its origins perhaps gave the population a sense of entitlement that worked in the empire's favour.

THE ROMAN KINGDOM: 753 BC TO 510 BC

Romulus ruled as King of Rome together with the King of the Sabines from 753 BC. It seemed the least he could do for having kidnapped all their women. They were succeeded by a series of legendary Etruscan kings – each of whom can be seen as analogous to other mythical founders in Greek legend, suggesting that they borrowed some of the Greeks' myths of origin and transposed them to their own Roman kings.

Some historians look beyond the myth to suggest that the series of kings we hear about from these early days are more likely to be clan leaders of the region who attained a certain level of notoriety for whatever reason. What we do know about this time, however, is that the society was already building on a perception of aristocracy, good family lineage and the succession of noble blood – values that remained ingrained in the society for many centuries.

It makes sense, then, that the succession of kings was eventually overthrown by a revolt of the aristocracy.

THE ROMAN REPUBLIC: 510 TO 27 BC

In about 510 BC, the son of the wonderfully named king Tarquinius Superbus made a big mistake by raping the daughter of local posh man, Lucius Iunius Brutus. This goes down in legend as the trigger for aristocratic revolution and formation of the Roman Republic. It is thought that similar revolutions against monarchic rule were taking place all over southern Italy at the same time, and the keen-eyed reader will note that this is around the same time as the first version of democracy was being introduced across Attica in Greece by Cleisthenes.

This gave Rome its independence from the Etruscan kings, and in time a structure of power was introduced. The original Senate was created – an assembly of aristocrats into which members were voted for a one-year position. They were overseen by two magistrates, a feature designed to prevent any one autocratic leader taking control. This gave the system of governance a level of accountability not seen before, albeit just among the aristocracy. The word 'republic' comes from the Latin *res publica*, which means 'public matters': the affairs of the state had become (in principle at least) the responsibility of the people.

As ever with such utopian ideals, the dream doesn't quite last.

Already by 501 BC, it was decided that it might be a good idea to have one *dictator* in power (not far off from the modern English meaning), in case there was ever a situation that required one man's decisiveness, paving way for the later emperors. It didn't take long for this to get to people's heads, and, between 444 and 366 BC, there seemed to be very few official consulship elections, and military leaders held those powers during this period instead.

Rome developed a fiercely hierarchical society not dissimilar to the feudal system of medieval Europe. Aristocratic landowners defined themselves as *patricii* (of the patrician class), and they made the rules. The *plebes* would work beneath them, surviving on the agricultural yield (or not) of the small patches of land they could get their hands on, with many suffering through extortionate debts owed to the *patricii*. The class divide softened somewhat as some *plebes* became richer, with the first plebeian consul elected in 366 BC. The plebeian politics was nonetheless kept somewhat separate from the politics governing the *patricii*.

WHAT'S IN A NAME?

Roman names generally consist of three parts. For example, take the full name of Rome's most famous dictator: Gaius Julius Caesar.

1. Praenomen: The given name or first name, Gaius.

2. Nomen: The name deriving from the clan that the person belongs to, Julius.

3. Cognomen: The more specific family name within that clan, Caesar.

This convention for naming meant that you could instantly see someone's social standing, with their lineage explicitly spelled out in their name. It is perhaps this that contributed to the rigidity of Rome's hierarchical social structure.

There were only about fifteen *praenomen* names in regular use for Roman men, and female names were often just feminine forms of these. Names were passed down to children from their father and mother, with girls often taking the feminine form of their father's *praenomen*. Gaius Julius Caesar was in fact the fourth person in his family lineage to have that name.

ROMAN LAW

The existence of this new thing called democracy gave the populace a sense of citizenship and a small degree of ownership on Rome's identity. In turn, it bestowed upon the state a sense of duty to care for its members.

In about 450 BC, a series of laws were published known as the Twelve Tables, which covered twelve detailed sets of codes of conduct and punitive procedures. The Romans were heavily influenced by Greek philosophy and governance at the time, and took many of their learnings into account. The laws were then engraved in copper and put on public display.

The excessive debts owed by many *plebes* were capped and punishments for nonpayment were regulated. That said, it's worth noting that the laws were written by (and for) the aristocracy, and that huge inequalities still prevailed. Marriage between the classes was briefly outlawed, and *plebes* could be sold into slavery as part of their punishment. The level of punishment for crimes also varied depending on the class of both the perpetrator and the victim.

The death penalty was restricted to the court room for the first time, and several of the laws gave more accountability to citizens for their environment: the condition of Roman roads was the responsibility of the nearest inhabitant, and all corpses had to be dealt with outside of the city walls. Some of the principles still exist as part of common law across the world today – such as the distinction between manslaughter and murder, and (equally critical) the liberty to remove tree branches that overhang into one's property.

While perhaps not comparing favourably to the human-rights code we have today, the setting-out of these laws for public display is a pivotal moment in Rome's history that transformed how its civilization developed – and how our own contemporary society was modelled.

THE ROMANS AND THE GREEKS

I could write an entire series of books just focusing on the centuries of wars that the Romans undertook, so for brevity it is enough to say that they were fighting continuously on all sides – in Italy, Hispania, Gaul, Carthage, Macedon and beyond. These were ongoing feuds that rekindled wars over and over again with the same enemies as well as new ones.

Rome had helped defend the Athenian Greeks against Macedon (Alexander the Great's successors) a number of times, and eventually had had enough and dissolved the state into four smaller powerless regions following the third Macedonian War in 168 BC. Clearly in a belligerent mood, it then turned on the heart of Greece itself in Corinth as well as old enemy Carthage and obliterated both cities in 146 BC, in two massive demonstrations of might.

This signalled the end of Greek independence, and everything that was Greek essentially became Roman overnight. Greece's history, culture, literature and religion had been deeply entrenched into Roman education and society – so the envelopment of this ancient civilization into the Roman Republic was something of huge importance. The wealth that came with such expansion makes this the time that Rome began to build its roads and aqueducts to connect the huge area it now covered.

SLAVERY

Slavery was all the rage in both ancient Greece and Rome. You can't look at a Greek vase without seeing the odd cup-bearer, sword-carrier or houseboy in the background. In fact, both the Greek and Roman civilizations owed a great deal to their huge slave populations, and would have had very little to show in terms of construction, military endeavour, infrastructure and empire growth without them.

Reports are sketchy, but it is estimated that some regions of Greece and the Roman Empire had up to one third of their populations made up of slaves. These were largely the spoils of the wars both civilizations waged on all sides: if your country was defeated, you could bet that large numbers of its population would be taken as slaves.

Slaves had minimal rights and were perceived (socially and legally) as the property of their master; they weren't able to own property, marry or give legal representation (unless under torture, naturally). It quickly becomes easy to see how even after the dawn of 'democracy' only 15 per cent of Athenian society was able to vote.

As usual, the Romans were able to take the Greek model of slavery and give it a turbo-boost: once they had control of the sacred Greek island of Delos, its strategic position in the Mediterranean enabled them to turn it into a slave market of unbelievable proportions. Attracting merchants from all compass points, it is said that up to 10,000 slaves could be sold in one day on the site – a task that would boggle the minds of even the most capable of market vendors today. Some reports even say that the port was specially built to allow boatloads of slaves to be emptied directly into the centre of the trading floor.

THE ROMAN EMPIRE: 27 BC TO AD 476

The first century BC was an unsettling time for Rome. Decades of dictatorships ended in the assassination of Julius Caesar in 44 BC, and power eventually was won by his great-nephew (and adopted son) Octavian following the Battle of Actium, in which he saw off Mark Antony's bid for power. The Roman Empire officially started in 27 BC, when Octavian took on the honorific title of Augustus Caesar, becoming the first official emperor.

It is from this time and throughout the first century AD that is known as the Golden Age of Rome, because this is the period of the most prolific cultural growth in literature, architecture, philosophy and law. Basically, anyone you've ever heard of probably did their thing around this time. The emperors who ruled during this time had mixed successes – the medically insane, incompetent or arrogant (Caligula, Nero) were interspersed with more popular emperors in Vespasian, Titus or Trajan.

In the second century AD, Trajan led a period of massive growth of the empire, extending Roman influence across the whole of the Mediterranean on all sides, ruling an area that covered modern-day Italy, Spain, Greece, Israel, Egypt, northern Africa, parts of Saudi Arabia, Iraq, Iran, southern Europe, France and England. He also continued the great advancement in construction and architecture across his large empire.

THE ROMAN EMPIRE AT ITS ZENITH

Such growth caused inevitable problems with governance, and, towards the end of the third century AD, Emperor Diocletian split the empire into two administrative regions (East and West), eventually creating two equal *Augustus* leaders, each supported by a junior *Caesar*. It is perhaps the presence of too many simultaneous leaders that meant this model was short-lived, and, by 306 AD, Constantine united the whole empire again, albeit amid a series of civil wars. It is around this time that Christianity began gradually to overtake the old polytheistic religion of Rome, creating yet more fractures and civil war in the fragile empire.

THE FALL OF THE ROMAN EMPIRE: AD 476 TO 1453

By the fifth century AD, the notions of East and West Empires were still strong, and leadership was governed more by military leaders than the (slightly) more democratic emperors. The Western Empire came under attack from Germanic armies from the north, and, in 476, the emperor Romulus Augustus couldn't rely solely on the heritage of his given name, and was overthrown by the German soldier Odacer.

Such extraordinary growth of the Roman Empire meant that it had enveloped many different nations and cultures, and it is thought that, by the time of the Germanic victory, the people of the empire had lost the central vein of Roman sentiment that was responsible for its initial success.

The citizens of the Eastern Empire (today known as the Byzantine Empire) managed to retain pride in a Roman identity for many centuries longer. It continued to assert its might across the Mediterranean, but was centred on the city of Constantinople (modern-day Istanbul) and Greece. By the seventh century Greek was reinstated as the official language of the empire (although it had obviously still been widely used in the meantime), but the Roman identity remained strong.

Constantinople eventually fell in an attack from West European Catholics in 1206. It was rebuilt, and a few brave souls kept the idea of the Roman Empire going until 1453, when it was finally consumed by the Ottoman Empire.

GREEK HISTORIANS: HERODOTUS, THUCYDIDES, JOSEPHUS

The study of history is not a recent educational development: humans have been fascinated by our past for as long as myths, storytelling and legends have been around. The Greeks started making more factual accounts of events from the fifth century onwards (although Herodotus has been known to tell a few porky pies in his work). The purpose is not just to chronicle events from a point of interest, but also to help future generations learn from the successes and mistakes of their predecessors: the study of history is crucial in our collective development as a society.

HERODOTUS

Herodotus was born in about 484 BC, and was given the title 'father of history' by Roman writer Cicero, since he was the first person to sit down and write a narrative history of events. His one existing work, *Histories*, is a celebration of the Greek victory over the Persians, and goes into quite some detail of the origins of the conflict between the nations, the details of their armies, and intricate details of the events of the battles. He referred to his work as ἱστορια ('historia'), which literally means 'inquiries', and from it we obviously get the English word 'history'.

Histories describes the rise of the Persian Empire, and the main events cover a period from 557 to 479 BC, following the key Persian leaders during that time. Later editors have split the work into nine books, each named after one of the Muses. The pivotal event is the Battle of Marathon, which saw the Persians defeated by the Greeks shortly before Herodotus's birth. When he was a very young child, Persian leader Xerxes restarted the war, but was finally defeated at the Battle of Plataea. It is perhaps hearing of these events as a child that inspired Herodotus to write about them later in his life.

Since Herodotus is mainly telling of events that happened before his birth, *Histories* still needs to be read with a critical eye, but his purpose (which he lays out at the beginning) is to recount the battles and to ensure that neither side forgets how the conflict came about. One can also assume that the mythological elements to some of the events are added by his own imagination, rather than necessarily being first-hand anecdotes. He tries often to include reference points and proof for events, to help give credence to his work. Despite that, Herodotus is sometimes known as the 'father of lies' – even by his contemporaries.

THUCYDIDES

Thucydides was an Athenian aristocrat born in about 460 BC. He was an army general in the Peloponnesian War, and pegged it to the countryside when he was sentenced to death for a military failure. It was in his exile that he decided to write a history of the war, and he was able to speak with people from both sides to get a fairer picture of events. Most critics believe he was able to compose a relatively unbiased history.

His work follows a rigid chronology, and goes into much more detailed theory than Herodotus on how the war came about, looking for the human actions that result in war, rather than attributing anything to the gods. The work contains many speeches written verbatim from Thucydides' first-hand memory, the accounts of others, or sometimes from a bit of guesswork.

The most famous speech is that of Athenian leader Pericles, who was speaking to his people at the funeral of the first citizens to die in the war. Pericles' speech is a rousing delivery that seeks to celebrate the greatness of Athens, the benefits of its democracy and the bravery of the dead. Thucydides is clearly a great supporter of the merits of democracy, but his work closely examines the behaviour of Greece's individual city-states to explain how wars begin, and he has a concern that the freedom and lack of strict regulation in the democratic model may lead to dangerous possibilities in the wrong hands.

In about 400 BC, Thucydides was allowed to return to Athens without fear of punishment, and it is around this time that his history comes to an abrupt end, indicating his death. One story claims that he was murdered on his way back to his homeland.

JOSEPHUS

Josephus is, strictly speaking, a Jewish historian of the Roman Empire, but wrote his histories in Greek, so we'll put him in the Greek pot. Born in Jerusalem in AD 37, Josephus originally was part of the Galilean revolution against the Romans. He was taken as a prisoner to Rome, and, in a bizarre turn of events, ended up being adopted by Emperor Vespasian and assisted the Romans in understanding the Jewish people. His works chronicle Jewish history and customs for a non-Jewish audience, and it is among these works that we have the first references to Jesus outside of the Bible.

In his *Jewish Antiquities*, Josephus speaks of the σοφος ανηρ ('sophos aner') – the wise man who taught the 'truth' to anyone who would listen:

> *About this time lived a wise man, Jesus – if you can even call him a man. For he performed surprising acts and was a teacher to people who received the truth gladly. He influenced even many Jews and many Greeks. He was the Messiah.*

– Translation of *Jewish Antiquities*, 18.3.3, Josephus

The word 'Messiah' comes from the Hebrew meaning 'the anointed one'. In Greek, the same meaning is χριστος ('christos'), from where we get the anglicized word 'Christ'.

This passage has remained a controversial piece of literature for centuries. Seventeenth-century Christians used it as evidence to the Jewish community of the existence of Jesus, who responded with the claim that words had been added by later Christian scholars in the third or fourth century AD. It certainly does seem like very effusive language to use from a Jewish writer, and a translation of an Arabic version of the text contains a similar passage about a 'wise', 'good' and 'virtuous' Jesus, but his status as 'Messiah' is only as reported by his disciples, rather than as direct as it is in the Greek translation here.

Recent studies have noticed that there are similarities in the Greek text of Josephus's account and with that of the Gospel of Luke, which was written about thirty years beforehand. This could indicate that later Christians took the Gospel as inspiration for a more 'Christian' version of *Jewish Antiquities*, or that both Luke and Josephus were using the same reference points from the earliest Christian texts that no longer exist.

No matter what your beliefs, Josephus's works are important snapshots of the rise of Christianity and the early conflicts between Jewish and Christian nations.

Chapter 3

An Introduction to
Greek Literature

Homer

BACKGROUND

The most famous name in Greek literature is also one of the most mysterious. If you go by what you're taught in school, Homer was a poet living in eastern Greece somewhere between 800 and 700 BC, and spent his days writing epic poems such as *The Iliad* and *The Odyssey*.

For those of you who were paying attention in Chapter 1, you'll notice that this means Homer wrote his works on about the same day as the Greek alphabet was *invented* – which is no mean feat, considering these two poems alone contain nearly 30,000 lines between them of this new stuff called writing. In fact, Homer's works are accepted as the first ever compositions of Western literature. And, if you believe the stories that he was blind too, then the mind boggles.

HOMERIC GREEK

So how did he do it?

If you read Homer's poems in the original Greek (no worries if you haven't got round to it just yet), you will notice that his Greek is a unique form of the language. It uses words and structures seen only in Homer's work – giving him his own 'Homeric Greek'. Looking at particular phrases, you can see that there are elements from several different Greek dialects all in one poem. In fact, the same word can sometimes appear in different dialects throughout his works.

Even more striking is that the different dialects used aren't only geographical: some of the inconsistencies in the language indicate that some passages were composed at a completely different time from others. It's like having one English poem with colloquialisms from Britain, the USA and Australia mixed in with a couple of phrases from Chaucer and Shakespeare, all in the same passage. And then passing it off as your own work.

This all points to the fact that Homer's poems weren't written down by one man on one hot Greek afternoon, but that they were actually composed by many different people from across not only a variety of geographical regions, but also across a long period of time. It is thought that the poems weren't initially written down at all, but passed on through the tradition of singing bards, who would travel the country singing works by Homer and other poets. And, as the stories were passed down orally from one to another, a game of Chinese whispers that spanned generations brought with it a unique form of Greek.

HOW TO RECITE 30,000 LINES OF POETRY

So the next problem: how on earth did these singing travellers remember tens of thousands of lines of poetry?

Each line was composed to a particular measure of syllables: each has six sets of syllable patterns, so is known as a hexameter. This is perhaps imperceptible to our ear, but this gave it a certain rhythm to your average Greek bard that would have helped to commit the poetry to memory.

When you read Homer's works in any language, you'll also notice the phrases and sentences that are repeated throughout each poem. In some cases, whole passages are used again and again. While at first this could seem like lazy composition, the repetition of the phrases actually gives quite a hypnotic and beautiful rhythm to his epic works. And in the tradition of the singing bard, this would have added familiarity and song to the stories – not only for the listeners, but also to the poor man trying to remember the whole lot.

And, incidentally, that whole thing about his being blind is probably just down to his name in Greek having connotations to blindness in some dialects.

SO WHO WAS HE?

It could be the case that Homer was indeed a blind chap from near the Turkish coast, who composed astonishingly beautiful poetry, and whose stories were passed from one singing bard to another, each adding his own regional twang. On the other hand, the poems could be an amalgamation of different folklore, fused together over time into one narrative. (That story about the singing Sirens enticing sailors towards jagged coastal rocks is one that crops up in different guises around the world.)

What remains is the amazing influence the works attributed to Homer have had on our modern world. Many elements from his stories, and many of the stories themselves, remain commonplace in today's storytelling and even in Hollywood movies – such as the war at Troy, the Trojan Horse, the Cyclops and the screaming Sirens. Our modern interpretations of these tales through film are just a continuation of that oral tradition, adding our own cultural references and language to the legends we have been told.

Considering these are some of the oldest stories in our

civilization, composed even before the invention of Western writing could preserve them, it is nothing short of astounding that they are still being told today across the world.

THE ILIAD

BACKGROUND

The Iliad is widely regarded as the oldest piece of Western literature. Made up of twenty-four books, it tells the story of the ten-year War of Troy (Ilium is the Greek name for the city) between the Greeks and the Trojans, with the main plot taking place towards the very end of the war on the plain outside the walls of Troy. Those who believe the war reflects real events place it as occurring in the twelfth century BC, so it would already be the stuff of legend by the time Homer got composing four hundred years later.

Like most key events in Homer's works, the war came about as a result of bickering between the gods, who decide to take it out on us poor mortals. The king of the gods, Zeus, gives an apple to one of the world's most eligible bachelors, Paris. Upon it is written καλλιστη ('kallistei'), meaning 'for the most beautiful woman', and Paris has to make the unenviable decision of who receives the apple among the three goddesses Aphrodite (goddess of love), Hera (Zeus's wife) and Athena (goddess of wisdom and courage, among others). It was never going to end well.

Paris gives the apple to Aphrodite, who rewards him by making the most beautiful woman in the world fall in love with him. The only problem is that this woman, Helen, is already married to a Greek king, Menelaus. Paris steals Helen away from Menelaus and takes her back to Troy. This sparks the beginning of the war between the Greeks and Trojans that occupies so much of epic poetry from both the Greeks and the Romans – including Homer's *Iliad* and *Odyssey* and Virgil's *Aeneid*.

WHO'S WHO

In the Greek corner, the key players are army leader Achilles; his young companion Patroclus; King of Mycenae Agamemnon; and King of Sparta Menelaus, brother of Agamemnon, and husband of the stolen Helen. In the Trojan corner, the army is led by Hector. He is the brother of Paris, and together they are the sons of Priam, who is King of Troy.

In addition to the mortals, the gods cannot be overlooked as playing key roles in the poetry. Their intervention and bickering are reflected on the ground throughout – negotiating with and outwitting one another to offer support to whichever of the sides each god is supporting.

GETTING READY FOR WAR

Most of the poem is consumed by infighting among the Greeks, with Achilles throwing the toys out of his pram because he's forced to return his captive prize Briseis. (It seems to be absolutely fine for the Greeks to take their own female prizes, never mind that the whole war was started over the taking of Helen by Paris.) He refuses to fight Agamemnon's war, and his mother asks Zeus to bring the Greeks to their knees so that they see how much they need Achilles in their army. The gods intervene and send the Greeks and Trojans into battle without Achilles.

Nearly half of Book 2 is taken up by the (very) lengthy listing of all the different contingents of both the Greek and Trojan armies as they prepare for battle. While not a fascinating read, it gives a sense of scale to the two entire nations about to clash, and makes the later battle scenes and loss of life much more personal. For the original listeners to the poem, it is also a great tool to get them engaged and excited about their regions being involved in Homer's work. It's possible that, in the tradition of the spoken poem, the list of regions and characters became longer and longer as it travelled around Greece from one bard to another.

GREEK VICTORY

Fighting commences. An initial Greek victory is called after Paris and Menelaus agree to a duel, but the bickering gods aren't happy with this outcome and the war continues. Several books are dedicated to the toing and froing of the gods' disagreements and the corresponding brutal loss of life on both sides on the ground.

Achilles is still refusing to fight, and in Book 16 his companion Patroclus goes against his advice and goes into battle wearing Achilles' armour. He is killed by Hector, and this news sends Achilles into such a rage that he goes into battle on a violent rampage, wearing sparkly new armour made for him by Hephaestus (blacksmith of the gods). He has a power and ferocity spurred on by his grief.

Achilles eventually faces Hector, whom he kills, and then spends twelve whole days brutally mistreating the dead body – most notably by threading a cord through Hector's heel tendons, tying him to his chariot and dragging him about for a while. Anything other than a proper ceremony and burial is seen as truly barbaric in the eyes of the Greeks.

He eventually sees sense and returns the body to the Trojans and allows King Priam enough time to give his son an appropriate send-off. This is where *The Iliad* ends.

ACHILLES AND PATROCLUS

Over the past 2,700 years, different societies have made different assumptions about the relationship between Achilles and his companion Patroclus.

Many early commentators in the fifth century BC onwards suggest the relationship is a sexual one. Tender passages and descriptions in the text could support this. The Greeks didn't generally condone homosexual relationships, but it seemed perfectly acceptable for an upstanding member of society to have a pederastic relationship with a younger chap.

More conservative societies play down the potentially sexual nature of the relationship, or omit it completely, as in the 2004 American movie *Troy*, which is based on Homer's *Iliad*. It doesn't matter either way; what remains important is the close bond they have and the motivation that Achilles' grief gives him to rejoin the Greeks' battle.

WHAT'S IT ALL ABOUT, THEN?

The Iliad's opening word sums it up quite well: μηνιν ('menin'). It is this anger that drives much of the motivation for the key figures in the poem. Pride and revenge are the starting point for the dispute among the goddesses, whom Paris has offended in his initial judgement with Zeus's apple. This then filters down to the mortal world, with Agamemnon and Paris (and two entire nations) set against one another in a fight for Helen.

Similar pride and revenge are seen in the war prizes the Greeks hand back to the Trojans, including Achilles' prize Briseis. His pride takes Achilles away from the front line, and it is only his rage at Patroclus's death that brings him back into the war towards the end of the poem.

The concept of fate is also important to Homer's first work, as a precursor to the unavoidable fates set out for heroes by prophecies in Greek tragedies (more on that in the next section). Hector, Achilles and Patroclus are among the characters who go into battle despite being told that doing so will lead to their deaths. The prophecies of course always come true – Achilles' death is not told in *The Iliad*, however.

Looking forwards beyond the war, the idea of homecoming is introduced as a set-up for the sequel epic poem, *The Odyssey*, in which the hero makes his long way home from the war.

The Odyssey

BACKGROUND

The Odyssey is essentially a sequel to *The Iliad* – and therefore the second composition in Western literature. The theme and structure are very different from that of Homer's first epic: we move away from war, honour and retribution and focus more on the journey (physical and otherwise) of a man learning from the mistakes made by himself, his men and the others whom he meets.

With this shift in theme, it is pertinent that the opening word of *The Iliad* is μηνιν ('menin' – anger), and that the opening word of *The Odyssey* is ανδρα ('andra' – man).

The new hero, Odysseus, has in fact already popped up in Homer's first epic as a noble soldier and a trusted member of the Greek army. Following the fall of Troy after the ten-year war, he makes his way back home to Ithaca in this second work. He gets a bit lost along the way, and takes about ten years (and 12,000 lines of Greek poetry) to get there, allowing for several incredible japes and moral life lessons along the way. The narrative is told in a nonlinear fashion, using storytelling to skip back over the ten years of his journey.

SETTING UP THE STORY

Back in Ithaca, Odysseus's wife Penelope is assumed a widow, and is plagued daily by suitors who have moved in and want to take his place. A bit of a wily sort, she uses delaying tactics like promising that she will pick a suitor when she has finished weaving a burial shroud for Odysseus's father. Each night she sneaks back and undoes some of her weaving, and manages to stave them off for the whole time.

Their only son, Telemachus (his name literally means 'far from the fighting'), is now a grown man and goes off in search of news about Odysseus from those who were at Troy with him. At every step of the way, the gods are ever present, and their intervention, their feuds and their anger are often the cause of a twist of fate for anyone on the ground. Athena seems a good sort, and keeps disguising herself as Telemachus, Odysseus or anyone else who takes her fancy in order to intervene. She is with Odysseus at every step, imperceptibly helping him along his journey.

Telemachus learns that Odysseus has been trapped on an island with the nymph Calypso (her name means 'the concealer') for about seven years following the end of the Trojan War. With Athena's help, Odysseus is eventually able to leave and washes up on the island of the Phaeacians, and it is here that he tells his own story.

THE CYCLOPS

Odysseus's extraordinary tale sees him battling amnesia, dodging cannibals and having his men being turned into pigs. He and some of his men are captured at one point by the giant Cyclops, Polyphemus, and are held captive in his cave. To avoid the fate that some of them meet of being gruesomely eaten by the Cyclops, Odysseus hatches a plan to get the giant completely drunk. When he is passed out in the cave, Odysseus drives a burning stake into his one eye, rendering him blind. Cunningly, he has told the Cyclops that his name is Οὖτις (Outis), which means 'No one', so, when the neighbours ask what all the noise is about, Polyphemus simply tells them that No one is hurting him. Inspired.

Odysseus and his men are able to escape by strapping themselves to the underside of Polyphemus's giant sheep, but, in a moment of pride (or hubris, from the Greek ὕβρις), Odysseus calls back and reveals his identity as his ship sets sail. In a terrible stroke of bad luck, the Cyclops's father happens to be Poseidon, god of the sea, whom Odysseus has already annoyed a couple of times before. Polyphemus calls up to his father, invoking him to ensure that Odysseus either never makes it home, or that he does reach Ithaca, but alone and to a broken home. We all learn a valuable lesson about not boasting of our victories.

(As an aside on etymology, Polyphemus's name is also worthy of note. In the same way that the English word *eu-phemism* comes from the Greek meaning 'speaking well of something', *Poly-phemus* can mean 'saying many things'. Polyphemus's words as Odysseus is escaping predict many things for the hero, and result in a much tougher return home. He should have known when they were introduced, really.)

ODYSSEUS RETURNS HOME

Odysseus's story sees him avoiding whirlpools, outwitting terrible creatures, visiting spirits and forcing himself to listen to the irresistible song of the Sirens (from whom we get the modern meaning), while his men block their ears with wax to avoid being enticed towards their jagged rocks. He also is compelled to be the lover of any number of beautiful goddesses along the way, which is deemed perfectly acceptable behaviour for a Greek man while your wife is at home weaving for twenty years.

Telemachus and Odysseus eventually make it back to Ithaca at about the same time and plot the killing of all of the suitors who have been hanging around since his presumed death. Athena plays a big part as always, and disguises Odysseus as an old beggar who is mocked by the suitors. Penelope is unaware of his identity and sets up a challenge that she will choose the man who can successfully string Odysseus's old bow and hit a few improbable bullseyes.

Odysseus is the only one who can complete the challenge, and then massacres the whole lot with the help of his son (and Athena of course). They kill a few of the house staff as well for good measure, and we can only assume Penelope had to sweep up all those dead bodies and get back to her weaving – although the text doesn't make this clear. His identity is revealed, and, after a few of the loose ends are tied up, anyone who is still alive lives happily ever after.

SOME USEFUL MUSES

In Greek mythology, the titaness Mnemosyne was the personification of memory, her name deriving from a Greek word for 'mindful', which is perpetuated in English words like 'mnemonic'. She was also the mother of the Muses, the nine sister-goddesses who inspire all the arts. This came about because she slept with Zeus on nine consecutive nights, and as a result – in a triumph of mythology over biology – gave birth to nine daughters. These are:

Calliope, Muse of Epic Poetry – symbol, a
    writing tablet
Clio, Muse of History – symbol, scrolls
Erato, Muse of Lyric Poetry (especially love poetry) –
    symbol, a cithara (an instrument of the lyre family)
Euterpe, Muse of Music (and later of Lyric Poetry) –
    symbol, a flute-like instrument
Melpomene, Muse of Tragedy – symbol, a tragic mask

Polyhymnia, Muse of Hymns – symbol, a veil

Terpsichore, Muse of Light Verse and Dance – symbol, a lyre

Thalia, Muse of Comedy – symbol, a comic mask

Urania, Muse of Astronomy – symbols, a globe and compass

'THE TENTH MUSE'

This was how Plato described the ancient Greek poet Sappho of Lesbos (*c*. 630–612 to *c*. 570 BC). Although most of her poetry, which was greatly admired in classical times, has not survived, her reputation has endured through the fragments that have come down to us. The scholars of Hellenistic Alexandria regarded her as one of the nine lyric poets, a list of archaic Greek poets spanning the seventh to the fifth centuries BC that included Alcaeus of Mytilene, Simonides of Ceos and Pindar. Very little is known of Sappho's life, and what is known cannot be considered reliable. Although her name and that of her birthplace gave us the adjectives 'sapphic' and 'lesbian', the meanings associated with female homosexuality (rather than with Sappho's poetry or referring to Lesbos) date only from the late nineteenth century, while the evidence that Sappho was gay is, at the very best, tenuous.

The concept of writers and artists – and others, such as astronomers – being inspired by Muses continued in Western art and literature for many centuries, as in the Prologue to Act I of Shakespeare's *King Henry V*, which begins, 'O! for a Muse of fire, that would ascend / The brightest heaven of invention.'

WHAT'S IT ALL ABOUT, THEN?

In experiencing the wrath of fantastical otherworldly characters, Homer is able to draw attention to the correct and proper way for a noble Greek man to behave, and Odysseus tends to learn something quite valuable about morality at each turn. It is the folly of his men, and actions of greed, pride and desire that guide the poem's ethics – and Odysseus indeed manages to lose every one of his companions before reaching home through these errors.

And, if you don't have the time to dedicate to reading the whole thing, the film *O Brother, Where Art Thou?* (2000) is based very roughly on Homer's poem – our own modern twist on the oral tradition of passing on Homer's stories.

I also cannot recommend enough the excellent translations of both *The Iliad* and *The Odyssey* by Robert Fagles (Penguin, 1990 and 1996 respectively). He has managed to capture the wonderful lyricism of Homer's works in very readable English that is a pleasure to read.

GREEK TRAGEDY: AESCHYLUS, SOPHOCLES AND EURIPIDES

BACKGROUND

While we may refer to many things as being 'tragic' on a day-to-day basis, the original term refers to a specific style of Greek theatre. Tragedies were led by a narrating chorus and depicted the devastating fall from grace of a hero, through which the audience experiences a cathartic lesson.

We still have complete tragedies today that were written by three Greek playwrights in the fifth century BC, and their influence on Western literature is immense. Shakespeare would have mustered only a few lines of poetry had he not had these ancient Greek masters to borrow from; and the influence he then had on modern literature, theatre and film would have been something quite different (*Romeo and Juliet*, *Hamlet* and *Macbeth* being just some of his plays that fall into their genre).

The original term τραγῳδia ('tragoidia') means 'goat song' from an amalgamation of the words τραγος ('tragos' – goat) and ῳδη ('oide' – song). There are a few theories as to why they were called this (either the goat was a prize for the best performance, or the chorus of singers wore goat skins, or somebody sacrificed a goat after a song); in any case, the meaning is lost on us, and may have been irrelevant even to your average Greek.

The key theme that defines tragedy is the inescapable fate of the hero or heroine. The gods usually have a meddling part to play, and prophesy some terrible destiny that will befall the principle character. In trying to avoid that fate, the hero falls headfirst into it, and the results are messy to say the least. And these weren't any old performances: many of them were held in the Theatre of Dionysus, which is carved into the side of Athens's Acropolis beneath the Parthenon and is still a phenomenal site today.

The versatility of the Greek language allows for the poetry of these plays to flow very quickly, producing some scenes of extremely fast and eloquently interwoven dialogue between characters. The tragic authors in this chapter were able to use their skill with the language to create some extraordinarily harrowing scenes that can haunt you for days. Spoiler: everyone dies at the end.

AESCHYLUS: *THE ORESTEIA*

Aeschylus was born in Athens in the sixth century BC and is often given the title of the 'father of tragedy', on account of his being the oldest plays we have of this genre. His most famous works are a trilogy of tragedies known as *The Oresteia* (since they focus on the house of Agamemnon and his son Orestes), made up of *Agamemnon*, *The Libation Bearers* and *The Eumenides*.

We've heard about Agamemnon in Homer's *Iliad* and *Odyssey* (composed a couple of centuries previously – see the previous sections for more detail), and the play in which he has the title role depicts his homecoming from the ten-year War of Troy back to the palace at Mycenae. He's a key player in the Greek army, and brother of Menelaus – who started the whole war in order to get back his stolen wife, Helen. Back in Mycenae, Agamemnon's wife Clytemnestra is less than pleased with the fact that he sacrificed their daughter Iphigenia in order to get a favourable wind for the Greeks – which you must admit is pretty bad parenting.

Agamemnon's imminent death is prophesied by his Trojan bit on the side, Cassandra, in a gibbering moment of insanity. No one listens to her, and both she and Agamemnon are killed by Clytemnestra and her new lover, Aegisthus. The play ends with the prophecy that Orestes will return to avenge his father's death. It's the ancient version of the phrase 'coming up in next week's episode . . .', as this is precisely what happens in the second play.

The Libation Bearers picks up many years later, and Orestes returns from hiding and finds his father's tomb outside the palace walls. He bumps into Electra (his sister, who wasn't sacrificed) in an absurd scene in which she recognizes him by their similarities in footprint. They plot to kill their mother and her lover, once Orestes tricks his way into the palace. He is initially moved by Clytemnestra's appeals for clemency (she even gets her tits out to remind him of their familial bond), but he eventually murders her, and is driven mad by the guilt. The chorus informs us, though, that this is not the end of the tragedy and to come back for more in the final part of the trilogy.

The Eumenides takes on a slightly different model, following Orestes' guilt as he is pursued from Argos to Delphi and to Athens by the Furies – a very spooky gang of spirits who want to take him to the Underworld for having killed his mother. In Athens, an improbable court case is played out, with Apollo defending Orestes and the Furies defending the dead Clytemnestra (I'd go for a trained barrister over this lot any day). Athena is the judge, and Orestes is eventually acquitted, ending the tragic trilogy on a surprisingly upbeat tone.

SOPHOCLES: *OEDIPUS REX*

Sophocles was born when Aeschylus was already doing his thing, and clearly learnt a thing or two from the master. They would eventually even compete against one another in tragedy contests – something akin to an ancient *X Factor*, perhaps – and Aeschylus did not always win. The ultimate flattery is that Sophocles rewrote and continued some of the stories that his predecessor had started, as well as adding many more of his own to the mix. The truth is that many of the stories were not original to Sophocles, nor indeed to the other playwrights, but their telling of them is what has stuck with us.

Oedipus Rex is perhaps one of the most stunning examples of tragedy. The Oracle of Delphi prophesies that the young baby prince of Thebes, Oedipus, will grow up to kill his father and sleep with his mother, so his parents understandably send him away to be killed. A shepherd takes pity on the baby and passes him on to be raised as prince of Corinth instead. When he's a grown man, Oedipus visits the Oracle and is told the same prophecy. Believing his parents are the guys back in Corinth, Oedipus pegs it as far from home as he can to protect them, and ends up in Thebes. (I think you can see where this is going.)

In Thebes, the turn of events sees him unwittingly kill the

king, and marry his mother, Queen Jocasta. Both Oedipus and Jocasta spend most of the play saying what a load of old tosh prophecies are – but eventually the truth of Oedipus's identity is revealed. The revelation scene is truly chilling, and will leave the hairs on your neck standing on end. Realizing that everything that was foretold has come true, Jocasta hangs herself, and, as Oedipus cannot bear to look at her hanging body, he gouges his own eyes out with her brooch. Nasty stuff.

Sophocles' work is the inspiration for Freud's 'Oedipus complex' (or for the naming of it, at least), in which he theorizes the desire of the growing man to want to kill his father and sleep with his mother. We're not here to learn about Freud, though, so we'll leave it at that.

EURIPIDES: *ELECTRA*

Euripides was a contemporary of Sophocles, and certainly would also have learnt from Aeschylus. Both he and Sophocles wrote plays called *Electra* at about the same time, based on basically the same plot as Aeschylus's *Libation Bearers*. Euripides takes a more light-hearted approach to this, and openly parodies the absurd recognition scene between Electra and her brother Orestes from Aeschylus's play – which would have been familiar to the audience.

Euripides' play tells the same story but from Electra's viewpoint. The play begins with her living a peasant's life outside of the palace walls. Following the murder of her father Agamemnon by her mother Clytemnestra, Electra is forced to live a miserable and very unroyal life so that she poses no threat to her mother's new husband, Aegisthus. Her brother Orestes rocks up after many years and, after his identity is revealed, they both plot the murders of the king and queen.

Clytemnestra is summoned to Electra's house on the pretext that her daughter is pregnant. Orestes and his mate Pylades meanwhile get into the palace and kill Aegisthus. Later, the brother and sister kill their mother and are racked with intense guilt. It is Orestes who strikes the fatal blow, but he has been encouraged by his sister, who even holds the sword with him. Their repentance and their realization that their actions can never be undone make the emotion of the play all the more poignant – and heightened even more by the fact that Orestes and Electra are forced to go their separate ways at the end of the play, and so can be of no comfort to one another in their guilt.

You can still walk around the ruins of the palace at Mycenae in Greece today, and it is quite some experience to walk through the very stone gateway that all of these characters are said to have passed through. Probably best to leave the family at home, though.

CHAPTER 4

AN INTRODUCTION TO
LATIN LITERATURE

Virgil: *The Aeneid*

BACKGROUND

The Aeneid is an epic poem commissioned by the first emperor of the official Roman Empire, Augustus Caesar, in 29 BC. Ten years later, the poet Virgil died with the manuscript not quite finished, and requested it be burnt. Clearly it wasn't, and it's a jolly good thing too.

Rome was going through a bit of a rough patch at the time, following years of external and civil war, a series of dictatorships, and then the collapse of the Roman Republic and rebirth into the Roman Empire. Augustus Caesar wanted a piece of literature to instil a sense of pride in the huge (and growing) empire of Rome, by telling the story of Rome's beginnings in a way that would make the populace happy to be called Romans. The poem also conveniently links Augustus by heritage to the very founders of the city, never mind that he was actually adopted by Julius Caesar.

Virgil took a lot of inspiration from Homer's two most famous works, *The Odyssey* and *The Iliad*. His *Aeneid* is written in twelve books, the first half of which tell of hero Aeneas's long and troubled journey away from Troy after it has been defeated by the Greeks. Aeneas is the leader of a pioneering bunch of Trojans who are to set up a new home in Italy, mirroring Odysseus's journey back from the same war in Homer's work.

The second half of the poem focuses on what Aeneas finds when he arrives in the new land: indigenous people who have to be beaten in a brutal war to enable Aeneas to found the city of Rome. Many of the details from Homer's war in *The Iliad* are reprised, albeit now with a more august and Roman sheen.

Virgil is clear from the start that he is rewriting the ancient Greek texts for a Roman audience. The opening line of the work reads *Arma virumque cano* ('I sing of *arms* and a *man*'), mirroring in Latin the opening words of Homer's *Iliad* (μηνιν, 'menin' – anger) and *Odyssey* (ανδρα, 'andra' – man).

AENEAS'S JOURNEY

Virgil's poem begins at the end of the ten-year War of Troy. The city has been defeated by the Greeks (Achilles, Odysseus and others among the victors), and Aeneas is leading a fleet of Trojans for a new home in Italy.

The goddess Juno (the equivalent to the Greek goddess Hera, wife of Zeus) is peeved at the city of Troy because its prince,

Paris, offended her when he named Venus (Aphrodite) the most beautiful goddess (see more on that at the beginning of the *Iliad* section earlier in the chapter). I know it's been over a decade since Paris made his judgement, and that Troy has been punished quite enough, but it just goes to show that you shouldn't mess with the gods.

Squabbling among a number of gods sees storms raised and stopped, and Aeneas and his fleet land instead in Carthage on the North African coast, where he meets its queen, Dido.

THE TROJAN HORSE

At a banquet given by Dido for Aeneas and his men, he tells of the fall of Troy with great emotion, neatly picking up the story where Homer's *Iliad* left off. This is our primary source of the legend of the Trojan Horse. Aeneas tells how the Greeks built a huge wooden monument and it was wheeled up to the city walls by one Greek, Sinon, who pretends to be abandoned by his comrades. He explains that the horse is an offering from the Greeks to appease the goddess Minerva (Greek Athena) and to say 'No hard feelings' about that ten-year war.

Unknown to the Trojans, inside the horse is a bunch of Greek brutes, led by Odysseus, and the entire Greek army has sailed away only to hide around the corner. Several Trojans warn against accepting the horse, but they are silenced, and a space in the city wall is created to get the massive offering inside. At night, the Greeks sail back to Troy and Sinon lets out the chaps who've been sitting inside the horse all that time.

The city is attacked, and amid the chaos Aeneas has a vision of Hector telling him to leave Troy. He does so, becoming separated from his wife in the meantime, but his son Ascanius and father Anchises make it (the latter being heroically carried on Aeneas's shoulders through the burning city). His wife is killed and later appears to him to tell him of his fate to found Rome.

AENEAS AND DIDO

The Queen of Carthage fairly quickly falls in love with Aeneas, urged on by some godly intervention. Venus (goddess of love, and also Aeneas's mother) is made to approve their love and conjures up a storm during a hunt, which sees the two seek shelter together in a cave – a scene worthy of any romcom movie.

But, ultimately, Aeneas is reminded by Jupiter's messenger Mercury that his duty is to found Rome, and that he must leave behind the love and carnal urges for Dido if he is to fulfil his fate. Aeneas explains to Dido in a fairly cold manner that he must go, and his ships set sail. In her pain, the queen prophesies an everlasting conflict between Carthage and the future Rome, and then kills herself using a sword Aeneas had given her.

The light from her burning pyre is seen by Aeneas as his fleet sails away, and he knows that she has killed herself. The emotive passages about her heartache and suicide make this one of the great love stories of Western literature. Aeneas later meets her in the Underworld and tries to explain his actions, but her ghost remains chillingly silent and won't look him in the eyes.

WAR WITH THE ITALIANS

The second half of *The Aeneid* tells of the brutal turns of the war between Aeneas's men and several indigenous people of Italy. I won't go into all the detail of who kills whom, where and how, but suffice it to say that the gods play their part in stirring up battles through pride, jealousy and sheer barbarity.

Aeneas leaves the Trojan camp for a while to form an alliance with the king of the Arcadians, Evander, whose people live on the current site of the city of Rome. So he returns with reinforcements, and a suit of armour and shield made by Vulcan (the Roman equivalent of Hephaestus, who made Achilles' armour in Homer's *Iliad*). The shield depicts the history (and future) of the Roman people in intricate detail – much of it making Augustus Caesar look intrinsic to its origins and success, of course.

Evander's son Pallas is killed by Turnus, king of the Rutulians, in a plot not dissimilar to that of Patroclus being slain by Hector in *The Iliad*. Indeed, at the very end of *The Aeneid*, Turnus pleads with Aeneas for his life when they are locked in a duel, and it is the sight of Pallas's sword belt around Turnus's shoulders that makes Aeneas strike the fatal blow.

This uncharacteristic lack of sympathy on Aeneas's part is

where *The Aeneid* ends, and Turnus's somewhat ungentlemanly death has left a bit of a sour taste on the origins of the Roman Empire among critics ever since it was written.

WHAT'S IT ALL ABOUT, THEN?

Emperor Augustus Caesar commissioned *The Aeneid* to be a fusion between ancient mythology, Greek literature and contemporary Roman values. Its aim was to give credibility to Augustus by giving him direct lineage to Aeneas, the founding of Rome, the city of Troy and the gods. Virgil invents an alternative story for the origins of the empire to suit Augustus's political requirements. So as not to devalue completely the existing mythology that readers would have been aware of, Virgil even explains that Romulus and Remus are direct descendants of Aeneas. The unbridled brutality of that myth (see Chapter 2) perhaps needed to have more depth given to it through the connection with Aeneas, in order to give Rome a more glorious origin.

Virgil uses Aeneas's travels and his experiences with some of the more barbaric Italian inhabitants as an opportunity to show characteristics that are distinctly *not* Roman. By his doing so, the Augustan view on morality is made clear. Several times throughout the work, Aeneas must battle between his emotions as a man and his destiny as the first Roman.

There is also a slightly darker side to the poem, which some critics have seen as hidden swipes at Augustus's methods. Most notably is Aeneas's uneasy slaying of a pleading Turnus in the poem's final lines. It shows that Aeneas wasn't always the morally upstanding citizen he was meant to be, and that he has a ruthless side.

Similarly, Augustus kept banging on about the state of *Pax Romana* ('Roman peace') during his rule. This phrase refers to the longest period of peace in Europe's history, but in fact belies the fact that there was a brief civil war and constant wars and land acquisitions on all frontiers of the expanding Roman Empire. There would be many people at the time who wouldn't quite agree that they were in a time of peace, despite what their new emperor told them.

ROMAN POETRY: CATULLUS, HORACE, OVID

While Virgil may have got most of the glory for Roman poetry, there was a very rich literary scene in Rome's Golden Age, and many poets who have been able to have their own influence on our modern literature in the way that Virgil did.

Catullus, Horace and Ovid each have very different styles, but all lived in the first century BC and have given us some of the most significant works of Roman poetry.

CATULLUS

Catullus was born in about 84 BC and we have about 116 poems that are attributed to him. He was part of Rome's high society, and could even count Julius Caesar among his close personal friends. He bucked the trend (and desires of his parents) by becoming a full-time poet instead of seeking a political or military career, and was able to find success very quickly, perhaps due to the style of his poetry.

Most of his poems are about love and sex, and he was not afraid to push boundaries. Worried that some of his more romantic poetry for his lover Lesbia was seen as a bit too clean-cut, Catullus seemed to enjoy tipping the boat with more racy writing. Translations of some passages are enough to make even today's readers blush, as he does not shy away from being very descriptive about what he might like to do to various recipients of his poetry – both female and male. Certain poems from Catullus's work have even been removed from school syllabuses, and publishers still need to think twice before putting all of his words into print.

So I think I should leave it for the inquisitive reader to search out translations of Catullus rather than risk quoting him here. In 1969, Celia and Louis Zukofsky published a homophonic translation of Catullus, with the intention of not only translating the Latin, but doing so in a way that sounds very similar to original Latin poetry. Quite some feat. The results are a bit garbled in parts, but certainly have some value as a form of entertainment.

HORACE

Horace was another well-connected poet. He was born in 65 BC and his family had all of their property confiscated following a civil war from which he is said to have fled in a very un-Roman act. However, he was able to redeem himself and was commissioned by Augustus Caesar himself to write poetry for public entertainment. He was even mates with Virgil, which was probably a good place to be for a poet of that time.

He is best known for his *Odes*, which are made up of 103 individual poems. They span all sorts of fairly regular social subjects (including banquets, wine, music, religious customs and women), and as such have been crucial in adding to our understanding of Roman life of the time. It is from his *Odes* that we get the phrase *carpe diem*: Horace is telling a woman (and the listener) not to concern herself with how she might one day die, and instead to live in the 'here and now' and make the most of each day.

Sapias, vina liques, et spatio brevi
spem longam reseces. Dum loquimur, fugerit invida
aetas: carpe diem, quam minimum credula postero.

– *Odes*, 1.11, Horace

Be wise, pour the wine, and, since life is short,
Hold back from long-term dreams. While we're
speaking, jealous time is fleeing:
Seize the day, trusting as little as possible in
tomorrow.

OVID

Ovid was born in 43 BC, and so lived in an age heavily influenced by Augustus Caesar's desire to create great pride in Rome, and he would have grown up with the great works by Virgil. Ovid's style clearly takes inspiration from Virgil, as well as from the Greek poet Homer and tragic playwright Euripides. He uses styles similar to Virgil – epic hexameter poetry as well as didactic works – but goes some length to parody the genres. While Virgil's didactic poetry instructs the reader on how to tend the land, how to keep bees and other useful skills, Ovid uses some of his poetry to instruct on the best way to be unfaithful and how to fall out of love. It is perhaps this maverick approach that saw him exiled from Rome in about 8 AD.

His most famous work is *Metamorphoses*, a collection of about 250 mythological stories all concerning metamorphoses of some kind, as you might expect. The gods are heavily involved with each legend, and the tales tend to give mythological explanations for the existence of certain plants or animals (it turns out most of them are the reincarnation of lost lovers, heroes or gods).

Ovid begins the work at the dawn of time and works roughly chronologically up to his present day. He takes the reader on a journey from the creation of the world, to the interactions of the gods, to the heroes of Homer's poetry, to the birth of Rome and Virgil's tales of origins, to the rise of Augustus. The poems are a rich source for our knowledge of ancient mythology, and end with the prophecy of a glorious future for Rome and the immortality of Ovid through his work – not a bad prediction.

The story of Orpheus and Eurydice from the *Metamorphoses* is worth picking out for its tragic beauty, and because it continues to influence works of art, music, opera, theatre and literature today. Orpheus sings of his grief for his wife Eurydice, and his music is so moving that it reaches the gods of the Underworld (Pluto and Proserpina), and they agree to return his wife to the world of the living. The only condition is that Orpheus must enter the Underworld to collect her, and must not look back at her at all, and may set his eyes upon her only when they have reached the real world. Orpheus lasts well, but at the last moment, he looks back at his beloved wife, and in an incredibly moving passage of poetry she disappears for ever. Orpheus tries to reach out and hold her three times – and three times his arms go through nothing, and she is gone.

Passages from Ovid's works have greatly influenced writers including Shakespeare, Dante and Milton, and therefore much of modern literature and theatre. Shakespeare's *The Tempest* even sees Prospero using a whole passage influenced by a portion of the *Metamorphoses* in one of his seminal speeches.

CHAPTER 5

PHILOSOPHY

THE PRE-SOCRATIC PHILOSOPHERS: WHAT IS EVERYTHING?

BACKGROUND

As the name suggests, the Pre-Socratic philosophers are all the big thinkers and philosophical schools that predate Socrates' game-changing approach (more about him later). This era of philosophy starts around 600 BC and continues up until Socrates and Plato were doing their thing about 200 years later. Philosophers who made their mark in this era include Thales, Pythagoras (yes, *that* one), Parmenides and Hericlitus.

It is worth noting that this was a different stage in the development of modern human thought; the kinds of things we investigate in philosophy evolve over time. Many of the Pre-Socratics took a very physical and literal approach to their philosophy, with their curiosity and enquiry being driven by a desire to understand the building blocks of the physical world. Today our scientific understanding centres on the fact that everything at some point started from nothing. For the Pre-Socratics, the opposite was the case, and they were sure that something had always existed. Or (in the words first coined by Parmenides) that nothing comes from nothing (ουδεν εξ ουδενος). It is only in the later stages of this era that philosophers began to focus on our own thoughts, behaviour and ethics within that physical world.

THE EARLY PHILOSOPHERS

The Pre-Socratics saw the natural world in a constant state of transformation: trees, flowers and animals growing, dying and regenerating. Such observations led these early philosophers to focus on existential questions of life: What is everything made from? What *is* everything? They were looking for answers about nature and existence without having to revert to mythological stories about the gods – something that got some of them into trouble.

Thales of Miletus kicked it all off – seen by many as the first Western philosopher. He, and the two Milesians that followed (Anaximander and Anaximenes), wondered what everything was made from. Thales' observations of agriculture indicated that water was the fundamental building block of the universe, while Anaximenes concluded that air was actually what made the other three elements of water, earth and fire. Anaximander went a bit more conceptual with a theory of the 'απειρον' (apeiron – 'the limitless'). He saw a perfect balance in the universe in which everything was made from this one limitless entity. The decaying and regeneration of the world either took from or added to this bigger thing. As I said: quite conceptual.

WHAT THE FLUX?

Following this was Parmenides, who thought that everything must have come from something else, and that everything had therefore always existed. He argued that all things remained the same but in a constant state of flux, and it was only our perception of them that changed. He was the first to call into question human perception of the world. His theory of rationalism argued that there was an ultimate truth of how things worked (λογος – logos, literally 'the word'), which was contrary to what we perceived of that truth (δοξα – doxa, 'perception'). In modern scientific enquiry, we develop our theory and use observation to confirm it. Parmenides did the opposite: he was committed to believing the rational theory (or truth), no matter if we mere humans observed otherwise. (In fact, it is possible that an early refutation of Parmenides' argument led to the development of atomic theory by a chap called Leucippus, but that's not for now.)

Around the same time, Hericlitus had a variation of this theory. He described the physical state of flux as being like wading in a river: everything constantly changes in the same way as you will never stand in the same water twice. He said you both are and are not in the same water. So this is contrary to Parmenides, who said everything remained the same and that we were not to trust our perceptions of change.

In any case, it's safe to say that the Pre-Socratics enjoyed getting their knickers in a twist about the paradoxes of whether something *was* or *wasn't* what you thought it was.

ZENO'S PARADOXES

The best at these paradoxes was Zeno, whose life spanned both the end of Parmenides' and the early part of Socrates'. He devised a series of absurd but tricky scenarios that used the concepts of infinity and rationalism to create existential paradoxes. For example, a man getting from A to B will first need to cover half of the distance. From there, he'll need to cover half of the remaining distance, and from there half the remaining distance again, and so on. This leads to an infinite number of tasks to be completed to reach point B, and so he can logically never actually get there. (He's probably too busy measuring distances.)

Obviously the scenarios can be disproven (most notably by walking across the room), but his paradoxes represent a development of the Pre-Socratic thinking from the natural origins of the world, to questioning what we know of it and questioning our own guiding truths.

WHAT'S IT ALL ABOUT, THEN?

What we see with all of these philosophers is a desire to understand what we are all made from and to explore the physical existence of the world. Their fascination with the decay and regeneration of the world could have stemmed from a morbid curiosity into their own decay.

While some of their ideas on physics may seem basic to us, their search for the fundamental building blocks of the universe is the same curiosity as is driving our own science and existential philosophy now. We have the benefit of technology to help us identify elements of the atoms and particles around us, and so we continue to explore deeper into the behaviour of ever smaller components of those particles. Simultaneously, we're extending our reach out beyond the whole Earth into space to investigate the origins of the whole universe. In gaining ever more detailed understanding of the physical existence of things, we can know our own place within the universe.

It is this physical understanding of what is around us that the Pre-Socratics were first to investigate, and our own scientific development is merely an evolution of that enquiry.

SOCRATES AND PLATO

BACKGROUND

Socrates was a philosopher born in Athens in about 470 BC, and he is said to have spent his days discussing philosophical problems with just about anyone he met, challenging their perceptions of the world. The identity of Greece as one cultural entity was emerging, and with it arose questions of how man should live his life within a unified society. While the Pre-Socratic philosophers busied themselves trying to work out what everything was made of and how it worked, Socrates and those who followed him were more concerned with their place in the social structure of Athens and the right way to go about things as a decent member of the community.

Despite being one of the most influential thinkers of the ancient world, Socrates never wrote a word. His teachings remain predominantly through the writings of his pupil Plato, who wrote many works that chronicle the dialogues Socrates would have with his (sometimes unwitting) students. Socrates never accepted payment for his teaching, and was opposed to the Sophists, who did charge for their education. He saw it more as his duty to help others look beyond their everyday thoughts.

Socrates' method was constantly to challenge preconceptions. He questioned his interlocutors' statements through cross-examination until the very basis of their beliefs had been dissected, interrogated and proven to be false (or at least not strictly true). Plato's reporting of these dialogues allows the reader to be taken on the same philosophical journey from believing a particular statement to realizing that it in fact cannot be true.

Socrates' methods eventually got him into hot water. Politicians and thinkers in Athens didn't appreciate this eccentric challenging the very morality and wisdom of Athenian society. In 399 BC, Socrates was put on trial for corrupting the city's youth and for questioning the existence of the Greek gods. He was sentenced to death by poison – a punishment he accepted with considerable grace.

WHAT IS 'GOOD'?

Given that our only knowledge of Socrates' teachings is through the writings of Plato (and others), it's worth bearing in mind that the philosophy and opinions attributed to Socrates have been tainted by the beliefs of the writers. That said, these writings are all that we have, and as such they have had a profound effect on the development of Western thinking, no matter whose actual words they were.

There are a few common principles that run through many of Plato's dialogues of Socrates. He proposed that man always acts on what he thinks is the right thing to do. It is the individual's morality and motivations that make him define the 'right' course of action in any situation. Because of this, many of the dialogues delve into definitions of virtue and what it is to be good, with the aim of helping the listener (and reader) work out what is the correct way to live and behave within Athenian society.

In his cross-examining method, Socrates tends to take a stance of ignorance. He famously said that the one thing he knows is that he knows nothing – and it was the awareness of his own ignorance that made him the wisest man in Athens. This position of ignorance allows him to dissect seemingly very basic statements and reduce them to their very building blocks.

It also gives him licence to end some of his dialogues in a state of inconclusive confusion. That's not to say they aren't resolved, but that they act as a demonstration of the complexities of adopting any single stance on a statement, as further interrogation can always be found to bring their validity into question.

THE REPUBLIC

One of Plato's most seminal works is Πολιτεια (*Politeia*), written in about 380 BC. The Greek word means 'citizenship', and is translated as 'The Republic'. In it, Socrates concerns himself with the definition of justice – what it means to be 'just' as part of a societal structure, and what it means to be a 'just' individual.

In a wonderful passage, the beginnings of a society are imagined – building up from a rural community to a huge city-state. Through this, Socrates and his interlocutors are able to propose how the perfect state should be structured. He imagines three classes of citizen for the perfect balance. The bulk of the population would be the producers – farmers, builders and craftsmen – supported by the auxiliary warriors, with the rulers acting as the guardians of the society. The same theory is mapped onto individual justice, with the human soul being governed by three principles: the desire and appetite of the producers, the spirited heart of the warriors that carries out the wishes of the other parts, and the rational ruling head. By matching principles against the body, the soul and society, Plato is able at once to discuss the right way for the individual to behave, as well as explaining the effect that has on the wider society.

Socrates uses allegorical tales to illustrate his point, and tends to get so caught up in them that they require reading about three times to understand fully what he's getting at. The best-known allegory from *The Republic* is that of the shadows in the cave. Socrates imagines prisoners who have spent their whole lives staring at shadows cast on the wall of a cave. They attribute meaning to the different shapes they see, and this is their whole reality: the shadows to them are real. In our world, it is only the philosopher who is able to investigate further to see past the shadows. Upon leaving the cave, he first sees that the shadows are cast by puppets and statues, and attributes a sense of reality to these objects. He is then taken outside the cave and sees reflections and shadows of the real objects that the puppets and statues represented, and eventually sees the real objects themselves. Finally he is able to look up at the sun, and realize that it is the source of all things and the reason he can see everything that is around him.

Socrates uses the analogy to expound his theory on forms:

that all things (physical and abstract) belong to some higher entity of themselves. This book you're reading is unlike any other book you've seen, but you know it is a book because it conforms to some principle of 'bookness'. The allegorical sun represents the quality of 'goodness' that defines all things within their categories. It's all a bit out there, but it goes some way to explaining why Plato preoccupies so much of his thinking with the definition of terms such as 'good', 'virtuous' and 'just': as a philosopher, he sees it as his duty to understand these terms as fully as possible and to guide others to their true meanings. With this understanding, it is then possible to make proper judgements about the right things to do in life.

Socrates uses the story to explain his idea of the utopian state with the idea that the only people who would be intelligent enough to rule in a fair way would be philosopher-kings. If you're as confused as I am about his theory on forms, that's probably the reason why neither of us is King of England right now.

CHAPTER 6

ANCIENT ARCHITECTURE

THE PARTHENON

Quite possibly the most iconic emblem of Ancient (and, indeed, modern) Greece, the Parthenon, is a dazzling white-marble, temple-like building that looks out over all of Athens and way beyond. It sits on top of the city's Acropolis (which means 'upper city'), the vast flat-topped rock that dominates Athens's skyline. Completed in an astonishing fifteen years in 432 BC, the Parthenon's architecture has been imitated countless times across the world – from the Bank of England to the White House. (It's a well-known fact that, were you to transport an Ancient Greek man to the Bank of England today, he'd think nothing of it and would wander in for a quick sacrifice.)

There is even a full-scale replica of the building in Nashville, Tennessee, of all places.

WHAT WAS IT?

The Parthenon was built in tribute to the goddess Athena, and housed a vast statue of the city's patron. The Greek word παρθενον ('parthenon') refers to the virgin goddess, whose statue we now know of only through later imitations.

Many Greek cities are built around an acropolis (the one in

Athens isn't the only one) – providing a safe natural vantage point and fortress, and therefore also the best place to house the most sacred buildings of a city. In the fifth century BC, the Athenian general Pericles went on a bit of a building spree and commissioned the construction of several of the Acropolis's most important structures – of which the Parthenon is one. It actually replaced a previous dedication to Athena, which was destroyed half a century beforehand.

Since its dedication to the goddess of wisdom, it has been used as a treasury, a Christian church, a Turkish mosque complete with minaret and a seventeenth-century gunpowder store (the success of which can be seen in half a missing side and no roof), and today it resembles something of a Greek construction site – although I'm assured that it is undergoing painstaking and meticulous restoration.

But, despite some decidedly unwise modifications, lootings and explosions, what remains is still a truly breathtaking monument to the Golden Age of the Greek Empire and one of the world's most recognized architectural achievements.

OPTICAL ILLUSIONS

The Greeks knew a thing or two about architecture. The fact that most of the visible damage to the Parthenon has been inflicted by human idiocy rather than natural degradation is a testament to their ability to build a sturdy structure.

What makes the Parthenon a fascinating architectural study is the fact that none of its lines is straight. Its architects (a couple of chaps called Iktinos and Kallikrates) knew that long, straight lines in buildings of this size cause optical illusions that would make it look top-heavy, and that would make the columns look thinner in the middle as an observer looked up.

They countered this with optical illusions of their own. The whole foundation of the building is curved both upwards and inwards – so the middle of the base is both slimmer and higher than at the corners. The columns around the perimeter are curved inwards at a subtle incline that would see them meet in the middle about one mile above the Parthenon roof – if you had enough marble of course. The columns also have a slight bulge towards the top to partially correct the unsightly effects of perspective. Similar features are found in other Greek buildings, but the sheer size of the Parthenon makes the magnitude of these optical corrections all the more apparent.

Some observers believe that the Parthenon's undeniable beauty can also be put down to its sound mathematical consistency (bear with me on this one). A particular ratio has been applied to some of its principal dimensions, giving it a visual harmony that is immediately pleasing. The ratio of the length of its base to its width is 9:4, as is the ratio of its width to its height. The distance between its columns is also at this same ratio compared with the column diameter at their base. Enough maths for now – but it's a satisfying theory to explain part of the Parthenon's instant appeal.

LOSING YOUR MARBLES

Now I don't want to ignite any sort of diplomatic situation, but we can't look at the Parthenon without mentioning the Elgin Marbles. This is the name given to the collection of marble monuments, friezes and statues that were taken with permission/stolen/borrowed (depending on whom you speak to) by Lord Elgin between 1801 and 1805.

Elgin was the British ambassador to the Ottoman Empire, living in what is now Istanbul, and is said to have received permission from the ruling Sultan of Turkey to remove some of the monuments that remained in the Parthenon and other buildings on the Acropolis. About half of the building's original monuments had been damaged or lost over the course of the preceding 2,200 years, so Elgin saw no problem in taking half of what remained in 1801 over to London. There was some contention even in the UK at the time, but they were then bought from him by the British Museum shortly afterwards, which is where they still are on view today.

The museum retains a delightfully stiff upper lip when asked about the marbles, and the less you ask about their infamous 1930s clean-up operation, the better. Archaeologists have discovered the faintest remnants of dyes on monuments at the Parthenon, showing that the original friezes were painted in brilliant red, blue and green – a far cry from the white gleaming faces we (and 1930s restorers) might assume they should be.

In any case, monuments from the Parthenon are scattered in museums across Europe – including Athens itself – and between them attract tens of millions of visitors a year to experience some of its beauty. The great edifice experienced centuries of neglect, but is now part of a protected world heritage site, receiving the respect this truly overwhelming building deserves.

KNOWING YOUR COLUMNS

Greek architectural design of important buildings like temples and markets was largely divided into three schools of thought: the Doric, Ionic and Corinthian orders. They can be very quickly identified by the style of the column capitals (the head or top, where the column meets the roof).

However, the orders have distinctive characteristics that go beyond just the columns – each one has a specific law of proportions and ratios linked to column width and height that defines the sizing or spacing of the roof, the windows, and other features of the building. Having said that, some architects played fast and loose with the rules, allowing themselves to use one order for a building's exterior and another for the interior.

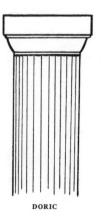  

DORIC　　　　**IONIC**　　　　**CORINTHIAN**

DORIC ORDER

The features of the Doric Order begin to be seen in Greek architecture from the start of the seventh century BC. It is defined by its simplicity: the columns are sturdy and with minimal decoration to the column capital and no column base. With a height seven times its diameter, the Doric column is comparatively short and squat. The 'entablature' that the columns support consists, in ascending order, of the architrave (resting on the capitals) with, above it the frieze and above that the cornice, with the pediment – the triangular 'roof' that is a common feature of classical Greek architecture – above that. The frieze may be plain, but is often decorated with low-relief carvings in the stone.

The Parthenon in Athens is in part the perfect example of Doric simplicity. However, when a building has been imitated down the centuries and across the world (see Federal Hall on Wall Street, New York, for starters; or the full-scale replica in Nashville, Tennessee, built in 1897), recent architects have favoured columns in the more ornate Corinthian style – even though this was by far the least favoured of the classical age. If you're going to all that effort, you may as well make it as fancy as possible, I suppose.

IONIC ORDER

The Ionic Order was developed in Ionia – on the western coast of what is now Turkey, which had been settled by Ionian Greeks – in the sixth century BC. The column shafts of this order are more slender, with a height eight times their diameter, and they have more vertical grooves than the Doric column. They are instantly recognizable by the four spiral scrolls at the column's capital, which have been likened to animal horns, shells and scrolls. They are called 'coiled volutes', but I'm sure that most architects secretly call them 'twirly bits'.

CORINTHIAN ORDER

The last of the Greek orders was unsurprisingly developed in Corinth. It is attributed to architect Callimachus, who visited the city in the fifth century BC and saw acanthus leaves growing over a basket of toys on a young girl's grave. The unfurling leaves decorate the capital of the Corinthian column, which stands at a height of nine times its diameter. The Romans also developed what came to be called the 'Composite Order', in which the column's capital features both the volutes of the Ionic and the acanthus leaves of the Corinthian. Composite columns appeared in Rome in the first century AD, but became more popular during the Renaissance; before then it had merely been considered a development of the Corinthian, rather than an order in its own right.

THE COLOSSEUM

The Colosseum is possibly the most recognized architectural achievement of the Roman Empire. Much of the round amphitheatre still stands in the centre of Rome today, damaged, of course, by the passing of time and earthquakes, but nonetheless a phenomenal monument to the incredible ingenuity of the Romans. The structure allows for an incredibly vivid insight into the culture of Rome in the heyday of its Golden Age.

BACKGROUND

The massive stadium was commissioned by the emperor Vespasian in AD 72. In a deft move to dissociate himself from the unpopular Nero (who had killed himself in 68 AD), Vespasian knocked down Nero's ostentatious *Domus Aurea* ('golden home') to make space for an arena for the people in the centre of the city.

The only thing that remained from Nero's pile was the *Colossus Neronis* ('Colossus of Nero') – a huge bronze statue of the former emperor that used to dominate the palatial home. It is possible that the moniker for the stadium is derived from this, as the statue was placed near to the new building, with its head and accessories being changed over the years depending on who was popular that year.

WHAT WAS IT USED FOR?

Private promoters put on shows at the Colosseum for spectators from all levels of society – from the city's poorest *plebes* (from which we get 'plebeian') in the upper tiers, to the very wealthy in the lower tiers, and the Emperor in his private box. And, from its inaugural games, the Colosseum clearly meant business: it is said that nine thousand wild animals were killed in these opening shows alone. I imagine that you wouldn't want to be sitting in the first few rows back then.

Some shows saw wild and fantastical animals like lions, elephants, rhinoceroses, bears and giraffes walking among constructed forest landscapes of real trees and temporary buildings. These often became elaborate and bloody hunting scenes, leaving the sand that covered the floor to soak up most of the blood – and for this reason it is from the Latin *harena* ('sand') that we get the word 'arena'.

Other shows depicted mythological stories or re-enacted battles. Often, dispensable slaves or criminals would be used to make the fights to the death all the more realistic, if not entirely real. Gladiators were often pitted against one another to a gruesome end. When not quite dead, the evident loser could appeal to the crowd and Emperor for mercy. If he was deemed to have fought well, the emperor or other dignitary could give the thumbs-down to signal he should not be killed. The motion of the thumb up across the throat signalled a less pleasant (but probably far more entertaining) end. These gestures are still used widely across the world today, even if we have upturned the meaning.

ROME'S BIGGEST SPORTS ARENA

The Colosseum is said to have had the capacity for upwards of fifty thousand spectators – about as many as the Yankee Stadium in New York. And not only would it rival some of today's biggest arenas for size, but some of its crowd-management features are also still not bettered nearly two thousand years later.

The rigidly hierarchical seating tiers across four levels meant that all ranks of Roman society could enjoy the shows that were put on. The huge stadium had a footprint of about six acres, and something in the region of eighty entrances around its outside wall. Spectators were given bits of old pottery with the exact block, row and seat number to make it as quick as possible to seat everyone. And the way out was just as quick, with large arteries exiting the building at all sides, called *vomitoria*, which is the same name used for stadium exits today.

(Incidentally, *vomitoria* were named so because they emitted people quickly, and had nothing to do with the misconception that Romans enjoyed regurgitating their food after a meal out. This was not common practice.)

SOME VERY CLEVER FEATURES

One of the most astonishing features of the Colosseum is the *velarium*. This was a huge awning that was suspended to simultaneously shade a large portion of the audience or protect them from rain, while being angled at a position that helped generate a breeze inside the arena. (The guys at Wimbledon Tennis Club have only in the last few years figured out how to use a retractable roof.)

Below the flat sandy floor of the arena was the two-storey maze of the *hypogeum* (literally 'underground'). This was used to house the vast number of animals and gladiators in cages and cells before they were due to fight. This allowed some of the more belligerent animals to be elevated straight onto the arena floor, and so saving the difficulty of leading an angry rhinoceros on a leash through the corridors.

The underground system also led straight into the gladiatorial schools and animal enclosures outside of the Colosseum, as well as allowing the emperor to leave without having to elbow his way through the queue for the hotdog stand.

It is even said that the structure was used to host re-enactments of bloody sea battles by filling the central arena with water and warships. Many dispute this, questioning how the site would be kept watertight, and it is suggested it was in fact another amphitheatre down the road that put on such events. An impressive feat, no matter where it was hosted – you certainly wouldn't get that past the Wimbledon Tennis Club.

The Colosseum is a wonderful architectural achievement, and gives a colourful snapshot of the culture of Roman society at the time is was built. It continued to be used in its original purpose for some five hundred years before Christian sensibilities deemed it a touch barbaric. Nevertheless, its influence on the way we watch sport and live concerts remains apparent across the world.

CHAPTER 7

SCIENCE AND TECHNOLOGY

Pythagoras

Pythagoras lived on the island of Samos in Greece in the sixth century BC, and his legacy will be common knowledge to anyone who was paying attention in maths class. The theorem that bears his name may have millions of children around the world asking what the point of maths is, but it is used constantly in architecture, astronomy, geology, distance measurement and other geometric applications beyond my comprehension.

Beyond his penchant for numbers and triangles, Pythagoras was also a philosopher, an astronomer, a priest in Egypt, the leader of a religious order in Italy, and a vegetarian.

PHILOSOPHY

Pythagoras had the good fortune to be around at the same time as Thales – regarded as the first Western philosopher. He visited Thales and his student Anaximander (more on them in Chapter 5) and was undoubtedly influenced by their teachings. Part of their studies involved cosmology and they are said to have been influential in his decision to spend much of his young adult life as a priest in Egypt to explore these disciplines further.

He eventually set up a philosophical school on Samos, and then, in about 520 BC (dates vary), he travelled to Croton in Southern Italy and set up an institution that was part religious sect, part philosophy school. All students were sworn to a strict secrecy, and were split into two levels: the inner circle of μαθηματικοι ('mathematikoi' – the learners) who were privy to much closer study with Pythagoras, and the outer circle of ακουσματικοι ('akousmatikoi' – the listeners).

Followers of his teachings lived a strict life with no possessions and a plain vegetarian diet, and thought Pythagoras was chums with all the gods. One local was so keen to join the school that he waged an attack on it when refused access around 500 BC, which led to the deaths of many of its inhabitants. It is said that Pythagoras fled to Metapontium, where he died not long afterwards.

MATHEMATICS

The Pythagoras theorem states that, for a right-angled triangle, the square on the hypotenuse is equal to the sum of the squares on the other two sides. Or, as it has been simplified: $a^2 + b^2 = c^2$

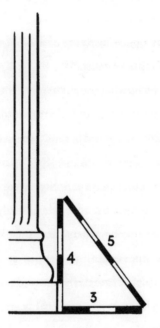

PYTHAGORAS'S THEOREM

The theorem was known before Pythagoras's time: the Babylonians were using it some one thousand years before him. However, it is Pythagoras (or perhaps the followers in his philosophical schools) who offered geometric proof of why the theorem is true. I won't bore you (and myself) to tears by trying to explain how he might have done this – but suffice it to say he was right.

The Pythagoreans are also credited with the definitions and construction of regular geometric shapes, different types of triangle and discovering irrational numbers. The less said about them the better.

Pythagoras barely separated his philosophy from his number-crunching, and considered that everything in the universe could be broken down mathematically. He assigned personalities and attributes to different numbers – giving them gender and degrees of beauty. Rather than sitting about doing sums, his schools would discuss what it is that makes a triangle, or the very nature of numbers. Defining types of triangle now might seem very simple, but, if you're the first person to give it a go, it is quite a feat.

PYTHAGORAS'S INFLUENCE

Outside of the classroom, Pythagoras's influence has been extraordinary. The principle behind the theorem he proved has countless uses for our measurement of buildings, geology and the universe.

His mathematical philosophy also stretched into music theory, devising principles around how to tune strings by their length and find perfect harmonies through mathematical ratios. He then even transposed this theory of harmony onto the spheres of the Earth and other planets to explain how the universe rotated around us in orbital resonance. His use of numbers and mathematical theory in philosophy and in the way he sought to understand the world also had a huge influence on the theory of numerology.

HUMBLE PI

Pi (π) is the extraordinary number that has mathematicians and numerophobes alike scratching their heads. Famously, it is the number that defines the relationship between the circumference (C) of a circle and its diameter (D), thus: $C = \pi D$ or $C = 2\pi R$, where R is the radius. (There are many other formulae involving pi, such as πR^2 for the area of a circle, but they all originate with $C = \pi D$.) As a constant, it holds a place of huge importance in mathematics, science and engineering, but also appears in many other fields that don't seem to have much to do with circles, such as quantum physics and cosmology.

First investigated by Archimedes (see page 171) in the third century BC – it is occasionally, though rarely, still referred to as Archimedes' Constant – it was accorded the Greek letter π by the eighteenth-century British mathematician William Jones in 1706, from the first letter of the Greek word for 'perimeter' or 'periphery'. It has an infinite number of decimal places, which never repeat. One enthusiast from Japan has even been able to recite the number from memory to over 84,000 decimal places. (Hilariously, the same memory enthusiast got up to 54,000 decimal places in a previous attempt, but had to give up when the building hosting the event closed for the night. The current record for memorizing pi is 100,000 decimal places.) Advances in computers in the late twentieth century allowed vast numbers of the digits of pi to be calculated, the current record standing at about 1.2 trillion decimal places, but I suggest you just stick with 3.14 or its fractional approximation, $^{22}/_{7}$.

Notable inventions ahead of their time

As this book aims to point out, the Greeks and Romans have a lot to answer for.

So much of our modern culture, societal structure and technology started with them. From the Greek legal system, theatre and literature, to the Roman alphabet, roads and aqueducts (some of which are still in use today), their influence on our everyday existence is immense. They even perfected waterwheels and designed the first steam engine – both of which weren't in widespread use in Europe until the Industrial Revolution of the eighteenth century stepped things up a gear.

The list goes on: books, coins, spiral staircases, maps . . . And the small number of inventions I have mentioned that weren't necessarily invented by the Greeks or Romans were certainly improved upon and brought into widespread use by them.

Below is a selection of some of the technology that it may surprise you to learn was invented over two thousand years ago. Considering that slaves were two a penny (or denarius), it wasn't as if there was a dearth of manpower to carry out everyday tasks for you; it seems that it was their desire to innovate, discover and teach that motivated such prolific technological development.

Vorsprung durch Technik and all that.

THE DEATH RAY

OK, so not quite the death ray of 1960s sci-fi movies, but not far off. Archimedes is said to have successfully defended the city of Syracuse from approaching Roman ships in the late third century BC by using an intense ray of light directed from the sun. It is not reported till a few centuries later, and scientists (and sci-fi fans) have been trying to recreate the weapon ever since.

As the ships approached the coast, Archimedes apparently trained a series of carefully placed (and very polished) copper mirrors onto them. The geometric positioning of the mirrors reflected and multiplied the sun's intensity, causing the ships to burst into flames. Apparently.

Several recreations over the ages have shown partial success, but the jury is still out. It seems that, to really get the fire going, the ship would need to be relatively close to the mirrors, and remain really still for a few minutes. Hardly the sort of behaviour you can request from a fleet of marauding Romans. And, given the close range required, you might be better off just throwing your shoe.

THE ALARM CLOCK

When your alarm goes off next Monday morning, I suggest you curse the name Ctesibius, if you can pronounce it correctly. In the third century BC, he went about making improvements to the ancient invention of the water clock that moved them from simple concepts to all-singing and all-dancing machines. Literally.

Water clocks had been around for millennia before him, and essentially consisted of a bucket of water slowly piddling its contents into another bucket below it. The passage of time could be denoted by the amount of water put into the first bucket. This design was used in Greek and Roman courtrooms and brothels alike to keep things on schedule.

But Ctesibius took it to a new level. He floated pistons on top of the rising water, which were attached to pointers to indicate the time more precisely. One design even attached the piston to the cogs on a dial, giving us the first mechanical clock face. He even invented ways to regulate the flow of water between the chambers using a floating valve, so that time didn't slow down as it had done with the more rudimentary design. The accuracy of time-keeping wasn't bettered for another two thousand years.

Through his designs, Ctesibius was able to preset different

mechanical movements when the rising water reached a certain level, giving us the first alarm clocks that would blow trumpets, drop a pebble on a gong, or make bird statues sing at a designated time.

Later that same week, he invented the snooze button.

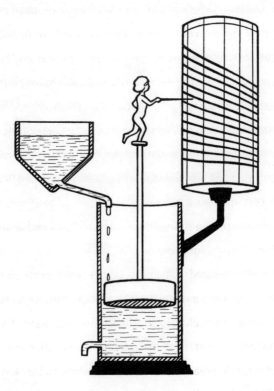

WATER CLOCK

THE VENDING MACHINE

Today's global obesity epidemic can be partly blamed on Hero of Alexandria, who was the first to design a coin-operated vending machine in the first century AD.

Hero was an imaginative and playful inventor, whose designs tended to focus on creating a sense of magic in temples. His designs tend to use water, fire-generated vacuums, heat and moving air to create the illusions of automated movement during religious ceremonies.

Among his designs is a vessel of holy water that would dispense a small amount of water when a five-drachma coin was dropped into the top. The coin lands on a spoonlike lever, which tilts open an aperture for the water to be dispensed. As the coin falls off the spoon, the aperture closes and water stops pouring. Simple, but genius.

He is also credited with inventing the first ever steam engine, which simply spun a metal ball round in circles, for mirth. Had Hero given this technology a little more thought, he might have hastened the start of the Industrial Revolution by a couple of millennia. Instead, he used the principle to make dancing models turn in circles, which I suppose has its own use.

AUTOMATIC DOORS

Apart from being motivated by sheer laziness, automatic doors were another spectacularly advanced invention by Hero of Alexandria. Once again, his motivation was to create a sense of drama in the temple.

His design describes lighting a fire on an altar, which then through a series of expanding air and shifting water in hidden tubes and chambers beneath the altar fills up a bucket concealed under the temple floor. The bucket is attached by pulleys and chains to the double door hinges and pulls them open, as if by magic. Extinguishing the fire allows the water to flow back to its original place, and the doors close again.

A truly remarkable invention for the age – although it would be a total pain every time someone knocked on the door.

Among Hero's other creations are the statues that are made to pour wine libations onto an altar when a fire is lit on it, and all manners of singing birds, blowing trumpets, hissing snake statues – all brought to life by hidden pipes, pulleys, levers and vacuums that are activated by something as simple as lighting a fire or pouring on water. The first ever wind-powered machine also is attributed to him – once again deftly avoiding any industrial progression and using it to power a musical organ.

SCHOLAR AND INVENTOR

'Give me but one firm spot on which to stand, and I will move the Earth.' So wrote Archimedes in the third century BC of the action of a lever, the man who was the first to state correctly the mathematical and mechanical principles behind the mechanism. In an age when almost all motive force had to be supplied by man or beast, or sometimes – as in sailing, or water- or windmills – by natural forces, the lever was to the ancients what the crane is to us today – an implement or machine essential to virtually any construction project, and to many tools such as scissors (invented around 1500 BC in Egypt).

Archimedes of Syracuse (*c.* 287 to *c.* 212 BC) was a Greek inventor, engineer, mathematician, physicist (who were then known as philosophers) and astronomer whose inventions included the Archimedes screw, still in use today for pumping liquids or for raising grain, among many other applications. His design of a block-and-tackle system used pulleys and the principles of leverage to move weights far beyond the lifting capabilities of human or animal power – it is said that, employing such an arrangement, he himself moved a warship loaded with men-at-arms with just his own strength and weight. This must have been, to use his own expression, a 'Eureka!' moment (from Greek εὑρηκα, heureka, 'I have found [it]').

CONSTRUCTION

Your average roadside construction site may seem a far cry from the streets of ancient Rome, but today's builders might be wolf-whistling with just a bucket and spade without some notable developments from Greece and Italy.

It is believed that the Greeks were using cranes in their construction as early as about 500 BC. Nooks in walls are found in some temples, positioned at regular intervals over large and heavy monuments and stones, indicating that some sort of mechanical winch could have been used. Many sites across the ancient world built before the introduction of cranes used much larger pieces of stone in their design, in order to minimize the number of times slaves or workers had to heave the building blocks up constructed ramps.

Following the mainstream introduction of cranes, it became much easier to quickly lift smaller segments into place – you just need to look at the difference between the heavy construction of the pyramids and the intricate placement of the Parthenon to see how the machinery changed what was architecturally possible over time.

Another phenomenal advancement was the Romans' perfection of concrete. The Greeks and earlier civilizations had used muds and fixing pastes of sorts, but by about 200 BC the Romans had developed an easily stored paste that would harden when water was added. This enabled them to build huge ceilings in one single piece, such as the one over the hall in Trajan's Forum – which is still intact from when it was built in 106 AD.

The Romans even perfected a concrete that would harden under water – transforming the construction of ports, bridges and aqueducts.

So the next time a builder wolf-whistles at you in the street while mixing some cement, try shouting '*Salve, amice!*' and see what he says.

HOW DID THEY GET THAT UP?

The pulley, combined with the crane, were two of the most important factors in any substantial building project in classical times. The crane was invented around 600 BC by the ancient Greeks, and, with the development of the winch and the pulley, relatively quickly replaced the use of earth ramps as a means of

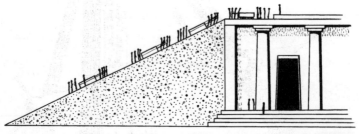

EARTH RAMP

raising constructions vertically. Aristotle (384–322 BC) is thought to have been the first to describe a compound pulley system, which allowed the lifting of even heavier weights; one of the advantages to the Greek city-states was that the use of cranes by small teams of skilled operators meant that they no longer had to employ large numbers of unskilled labourers, as had been the case when building using ramps.

BLOCK AND TACKLE

The Romans developed the crane, so that a *pentaspastos*

ROMAN CRANE WITH BLOCKS AND TACKLE

(see diagram on page 174; from Greek *penta-*, five, and *spastos*, originally from a verb meaning to draw or tug) using five pulleys and with four men on the winch could lift around 3,000 kg, or just under 3 tons. By contrast, in building the pyramids in ancient Egypt it had taken about fifty men to move a 2.5-ton block of stone up a ramp, using rollers, where the Romans were able to lift far greater weights with a much smaller workforce.

CENTRAL HEATING AND HEATED
SWIMMING POOLS

It's easy for us to stay warm and toasty in our homes with the flick of a switch. But the Greeks invented the model for the technique of central heating, which the Romans developed and made more widespread.

The temple at Ephesus (on the modern-day Turkish coast) is said to have used a heating system in about 350 BC. Air was heated by fires and circulated in gaps beneath floors to warm up the building. The Romans took this idea and made it mainstream, developing the hypocaust system for use in large homes, distributing warm air through walls and floors. 'Hypocaust' is from the Greek ὑπο- ('hupo') meaning 'under', and καυστος ('kaustos') meaning 'burnt'.

The same system was also used to heat large public baths called *thermae*, which started to spread across the Roman Empire from 25 BC. Fires lit directly beneath the baths made some so hot that visitors would need to wear special shoes to keep their feet from burning.

Advances in construction allowed aqueducts to carry fresh water to most reaches of the empire, with the development of concrete allowing the Romans to build huge vaulted ceilings to create bathhouses that catered for thousands of bathers simultaneously. These buildings also housed restaurants, libraries, exercise areas and something akin to saunas, and would put most modern gyms to shame.

Public bathhouses largely died out with the Roman Empire (it was deemed a bit inappropriate for the Christian sensibilities of the Middle Ages), and the principles of central heating didn't really return on a mass scale till the Industrial Revolution in Britain.

THE WATER PUMP

Not content with inventing death rays and discovering the principles of water displacement while taking a bath, Archimedes is also responsible for the earliest version of the water pump in the third century BC.

In answer to the inevitable amount of water that gathered in the hull of large ships, Archimedes invented a way to lift the water mechanically from the bilges back out into the sea. He constructed a large spiral encased inside a tube, so that each turn of the tube forced a small amount of water up into the next section of the screw, until eventually it reached the top.

Amazingly, precisely the same design is still in common

industrial use today for lifting both liquids and solids. Grain transporters and sewage drainers use the screw principle, and, when streams are diverted to flow down the screw in reverse, they spin the shaft of the pipe and are used as hydroelectric generators.

Although I do not wish this in any way to become an activity book, you can recreate your own version of Archimedes' design by taping a short length of hose in a spiral shape down the *outside* of a larger plastic tube. As you twist the tube, scooping up water from below, you will (eventually) transport water against gravity and probably onto your shoes.

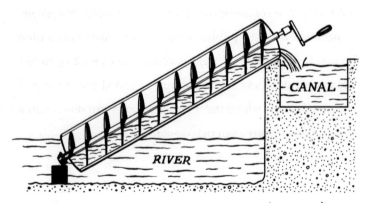

ARCHIMEDES' SCREW

FLUSHING TOILETS

Due to an unfortunate coincidence in his name, many associate the invention of the flushing toilet with nineteenth-century Brit Thomas Crapper. While he is accredited with the invention of the design similar to the one still used today, the concept of the flushing toilet has been around for thousands of years, and its use was adopted and spread by the Romans from 100 AD onwards.

By this stage their command of water was second to none, with aqueducts carrying water for hundreds of miles across the empire. So to divert streams of water to flow continuously beneath constructed toilet seats seems a relatively simple task – yet it is pivotal to the development of our concept of hygiene.

Romans created public toilets called *latrinae*, which housed long wooden or even marble benches with openings at convenient intervals. These were suspended over a covered channel through which the water constantly ran down into a sewage system away from the populated area.

GLASS

The use of glass dates back to the end of the second millennium BC in China and India, with evidence of rudimentary glass beads and decorative pieces in production. However, it was the Romans who took the art to the next level with the introduction of glass blowing in the first century AD.

Until that point, the production of glass was expensive and the results fairly uninspiring. Methods for injecting different colours into the glass had been common, but the results could only produce heavy moulded glass vessels that were probably as convenient as they were beautiful. With the introduction of glass blowing, objects could be moulded into shapes much more quickly and using much thinner glass – and therefore fewer raw materials.

Glass production became a thing of incredible intricacy and beauty, and by the start of the first century AD it was a massive industry that produced many household objects for the sake of both art and function. The Romans even invented glass recycling, using broken pieces in the production of new glass.

URBAN PLANNING

Many cities in America and across the world that have sprung up relatively recently construct themselves in a grid format, making navigation and construction easier for a larger population. However, the Greeks were planning cities in this way as early as the fifth century BC.

Miletus was a city of considerable clout, situated on the modern-day Turkish coast very close to the other big cities of Ephesus and Smyrna. It now lies someway in from the coast, having been detached from the sea due to the sediment deposits from the Meander River (the original meandering river that gives us the English word). It was once one of the most important cities of Greece, and it is the birthplace of philosophy, with Thales kicking off Western thinking in about 600 BC (see Chapter 5).

A Milesian architect called Hippodamus was one of the pioneers of the grid structure of urban planning from about 480 BC, devising a city layout to cope with a population of up to fifty thousand inhabitants. He even allowed for an unpopulated area in the centre of the city as a focus point for the society – an idea that can be seen very clearly in New York's Central Park and the open spaces that were kept free from construction as London developed.

SO WAS THERE ANYTHING THE ANCIENTS COULDN'T DO, OR DIDN'T INVENT?

Fly – the legend of the inventor Daedalus, and of what befell his son Icarus after he tried out the pair of wings that his father had made him, would have been enough to put an end to any ambitions the ancients may have had in that direction. But anything from their use of differential gearing to the theory that the Earth is a sphere, from the invention of the organ to vending machines and the odometer, point to peoples of enormous inventiveness and resourcefulness, as well as possessing that vital quality in any scientist, engineer or inventor – curiosity. It is sometimes difficult to escape the feeling that a Greek or Roman engineer, transposed into the twenty-first century, would need to take only one look at an F1 racing car before saying, 'That is about the most inefficient machine I have ever seen.'

ONE LAST GREAT INVENTION FROM CLASSICAL TIMES . . .

ANOTHER HUMBLE PIE . . .

Despite its established reputation as an Italian dish, pizza is thought to have originated with the ancient Greeks. A predecessor to pizza as we know it today, the ancient Greek *plakous* (πλακους) was a large, round, baked flatbread flavoured with toppings such as oil, garlic, onion, dates and spices or, according to some sources, cheese. The *plakous* might therefore also be a distant ancestor of the Greek pitta bread, which has survived the ages and lives on today.

With the Italian city of Naples as the home of the modern pizza, perhaps it is no coincidence that Naples, originally Neopolis, was founded by the Greeks in the ninth century BC. Just as the Greek name Neopolis translates as 'new city', so this new city eventually bred a new pizza towards the end of the nineteenth century, which travelled with Italian immigrants to the United States, and swiftly conquered the world.

The Romans also seem to have adopted a version of pizza, *placenta*, but using several thin sheets of dough, not unlike filo pastry, 'topped with cheese and honey and flavoured with bay leaves'. Cato the Elder provided a recipe in his *De Agri Cultura* (*On Agriculture*), the oldest surviving work of Latin prose, thought to have been written around 160 BC. A little later, in the first century BC, the Latin poet Virgil also appears to reference pizza in his epic poem *The Aeneid*, although the reference is hardly complimentary:

> *When the poor fare drove them to set their teeth*
> *into the thin discs, the rest being eaten, and to break*
> *the fateful circles of bread boldly with hands and jaws,*
> *not sparing the quartered cakes, Iulus, jokingly,*
> *said no more than: 'Ha! Are we eating the tables too?'*

– Book VII, 112–116, translated by A. S. Kline

It may seem frivolous to end this book with a note about the origins of pizza. It does show, however, that even now, after the passing of scores of centuries, our modern world is never very far from its classical origins.

Select Bibliography

All the books featured below are great introductions to the different facets of ancient knowledge that have influenced our modern world. There are, of course, thousands of books available, but I have chosen these for the keen reader who would like to explore a bit further any of the topics we've touched on.

LANGUAGE

Clackson, James and Horrocks, Geoffrey, *The Blackwell History of the Latin Language* (Wiley-Blackwell, 2010)

Horrocks, Geoffrey, *Greek: A History of the Language and its Speakers* (Longman Linguistics Library, 1997)

LITERATURE

Homer, *The Iliad*, trans. Robert Fagles (Penguin, 1990)

——, *The Odyssey*, trans. Robert Fagles (Penguin, 1996)

Trypanis, Constantine A. (ed.), *The Penguin Book of Greek Verse* (Penguin, 1971)

HISTORY

Chadwick, John, *The Mycenaean World* (Cambridge University
Press, 1976)

Jones, Peter and Sidwell, Keith (eds), *The World of Rome*,
(Cambridge University Press, 1997)

PHILOSOPHY

Gaarder, Jostein, *Sophie's World*, trans. Paulette Møller
(Phoenix, 1995)

Guthrie, W. K. C., *A History of Greek Philosophy*, Vol. 1: *The Earlier
Presocratics and the Pythagoreans* (Cambridge University
Press, 1962)

Plato, *The Republic*, trans. Desmond Lee (Penguin, 1974)

SCIENCE AND TECHNOLOGY

Hero, *The Pneumatics of Hero of Alexandria*, trans. and ed. Bennet
Woodcroft (Taylor Walton and Maberly, 1851)

Oleson, John Peter (ed.), *The Oxford Handbook of Engineering
and Technology in the Classical World* (Oxford University
Press, 2008)

INDEX